Stretchy Beans

Nutritious, Economical Meals the Easy Way

Millie Copper

Disclaimer

I am not a healthcare professional. I am a mom who believes that we are on the correct path for providing nutrient-dense, nourishing foods. You should do your own research and come to your own conclusions for your healthcare and nutrition, along with consulting a healthcare professional. I highly recommend contacting the Chapter Leader of your local Weston A. Price Foundation to ask about a list of healthcare providers.

This text contains affiliate links for Traditional Cooking School by GNOWFGLINS (www.TraditionalCookingSchool.com). If you make a purchase that originated from this document, I will receive a small commission. Your cost will be the same, and I greatly appreciate your support!

Copyright © 2020 CU Publishing LLC
ISBN-13: 978-1-7353101-0-7

All Rights Reserved

Material is not to be copied, shared, or republished without prior written consent of the author. All methods/formulas are original or noted as inspired/adapted.

Also by Millie Copper

Nonfiction Books

Stock the Real Food Pantry: A Handbook for Making the Most of Your Pantry

Design a Dish: Save Your Food Dollars

Real Food Hits the Road: Budget-Friendly Tips, Ideas, and Recipes for Enjoying Real Food Away from Home

Post-Apocalyptic Christian Fiction Books

The Havoc in Wyoming Series
The Montana Mayhem Series

Find these titles on Amazon:
www.amazon.com/author/milliecopper

Join my reader's club! Receive a complimentary copy of *Wyoming Refuge: A Havoc in Wyoming Prequel*. As part of my reader's club, you'll be the first to know about new releases and specials. I also share info on books I'm reading, preparedness tips, and more. Please sign up on my website:

www.MillieCopper.com

Table of Contents

Disclaimer 2
Also by Millie Copper 3
Table of Contents 5
Introduction 1
    How to Use This Book 3
    Nutrition 4
    Beans for Food Storage and Preparedness 4
Broth 6
    Meat Broth vs Bone Broth 7
    Making Meat Broth 8
    Making Bone Broth 10
    Perpetual Broth 13
    Vegetable Broth 14
Healthy Fats 15
Spices and Other Flavorings 18
Cooking Beans 20
    Soak First 20
    How to Cook Beans 21
    Alternative, Energy-Saving Cooking Methods 24
Sprouting Beans 27
    How to Sprout 28

- Baked Beans 30
  - Baked Beans in the Oven 30
  - Baked Beans in the Crockpot 31
  - Baked Beans on the Stovetop 32
  - Meal Options 1 33
    - Baked Beans 34
    - Corn Pone 34
    - Dunkin' Soup 35
  - Meal Options 2 36
    - Baked Beans 37
    - Breakfast for Dinner: Baked Beans Over Pancakes 37
    - Bean Chowder 38
- Pinto Beans 39
  - Meal Options 1 39
    - Pinto Beans and Rice 40
    - Bean, Cheese, and Rice Burritos 41
    - Layered Tortilla Pie 42
  - Meal Options 2 44
    - Pinto Beans with Cornbread 45
    - Taco Salad Platter 46
      - Sour Cream Salsa Dressing 47
      - Thousand with a Kick 47
    - Pinto Bean Chili 48
  - Meal Options 3 48
    - Pinto Beans and Tortillas 49

Breakfast Burritos	49
Navajo Tacos	50
Bonus Recipe	52
Taco Soup	52
White Beans	**54**
Meal Options 1	54
Fasooli	55
Crispy Pan-Fried Beans and Wilted Greens	56
Sauerkraut and Bean Soup	57
Meal Options 2	58
White Beans and Rice	59
White Beans and Cabbage	60
White Bean Soup	61
Bonus Recipes	62
BBQ Style Beans	62
Bean Stew	63
Creamy White Chili	64
Black Beans	**66**
Meal Options 1	66
Black Beans and Rice Platter	67
5-Ingredient Dressing	68
Stuffed Burritos	68
Curried Coconut Black Bean Soup	69
Meal Options 2	70
Black Bean Rice Bowls	71

  Chipotle Sauce 72
  Black Bean and Cheese Quesadillas 73
  Creamy Black Bean Chili 73
 Meal Options 3 74
  Easy Black Beans and Yellow Rice 75
  Black Bean Tostadas 76
   Ranch Dressing 77
  Creamy Black Bean Soup 78
Kidney Beans 80
 Meal Options 1 80
  Jamaican-Style Beans and Rice 81
  Enchilada Casserole 82
  Cowboy Soup 84
 Meal Options 2 85
  Rajma 86
  Southwestern Haystacks 87
  Sweet Potato Chili 88
Garbanzo Beans (Chickpeas) 90
 Meal Options 1 90
  Garbanzo Bean Curry 91
  Spinach with Garbanzo Beans 92
  Chickpea Tacos 93
 Meal Options 2 94
  Easy Garbanzo Beans and Rice 95
  Garbanzo Bean and Sprouted Wheat Dish 96

Hummus Platter	97
Hummus	98
Easy Tzatziki	98

Lentils 99

Sprouted Lentils 100

Meal Options 1 100
- Mujadareh 101
- Garam Masala Lentil Soup 103
- Lentils and Sweet Potatoes 105

Meal Options 2 106
- Smokey Lentils and Rice 107
- Sprouted Lentil Tacos 108
- Sprouted Lentil Patties 110

Meal Options 3 111
- Moroccan Lentil Soup 111
- Marinated Lentils 113
- Sprouted Lentil Bibimbap 114

Meal Options 4 117
- Friar's Lentil Soup 118
- Lentils and Dumplings 119
- Creamy Lenticchie 121

Cooked Lentils 123

Meal Options 123
- Lentils and Rice 124
- Lentil Loaf 125

- Lentil and Rice Burgers 127
- Whole and Split Peas 129
  - Meal Options 1 130
    - Whole (or Split) Pea Soup 131
    - Sprouted Pea Egg Foo Yung 132
    - Sprouted Pea Salad 133
  - Meal Options 2 134
    - Blended Pea Soup 135
    - Pea Curry 136
    - Pea Pâté 137
- More From Millie Copper 139
- Resources 141
- About the Author 143

Introduction

Are you looking for a way to stretch your meager food budget? Do you love the idea of making beans a focal point of your menu plan but worry about the preparation time? Or maybe you'd like to add beans to your food storage but aren't sure how to go about this. Or perhaps you already love heart-healthy beans and legumes but are just looking for more inspiration. Good news! This book will help.

My two most popular series on HomespunOasis.com are Stretchy Beans and my 13-Week Menu Plans—which features Stretchy Beans.

I was first introduced to the concept of Stretchy Beans over a decade ago through another blog. That blog—appropriately titled *Lentils and Rice*—shared many of her wonderful bean ideas. She'd make a pot of lentils and a pot of rice, then her family would eat on them for several days. I loved the idea and expanded on it. Sadly, the blog that was my inspiration is no longer around.

I'll admit, I was no stranger to beans prior to reading that blog. Growing up, my mama usually made a large pot of pinto beans on Friday night, and we ate on them all weekend. As a young (very broke) adult, I cooked pintos regularly and used the leftovers to make delicious chili. Yum!

When I discovered the Stretchy Bean concept, it came at a time when our budget really needed it.

We were in the process of switching to a traditional foods diet based on the ideas shared in *Nourishing Traditions* by Sally Fallon. In essence, traditional foods are real, whole foods that have been enjoyed for generations. The kinds of foods our ancestors may have eaten. The kinds of foods shared in the Bible. The foods Weston A. Price writes about in his book *Nutrition and Physical Degeneration*. Foods that were popular before our food supply was fully modernized and industrialized.

When I first started reading and learning about traditional foods, I was convinced eating these whole, real, traditional foods was not something my family could do with our modest food budget. A can of O-shaped spaghetti was cheap. A hunk of grass-fed beef was expensive. I was so overwhelmed with what I expected to be a huge increase in our food budget that I did nothing.

For months, I complained to anyone who would listen about how I wanted to start eating better. I was so sure the stomach troubles my husband and I experienced (we were both diagnosed with Irritable Bowel Syndrome—a diagnosis provided when they can't find anything wrong with you!) and my young daughter, only a preteen at the time, experienced could improve if we fixed our diet. I didn't think we'd be cured, but I prayed we'd find some relief.

I was so hung up on the idea of switching our entire diet overnight, I couldn't see the forest for the trees. Reading the *Lentils and Rice* blog sparked a memory in me. *Nourishing Traditions* has an entire chapter devoted to legumes!

While boring and unexciting compared to raw milk, grass-fed meats, and organic produce, I returned to the chapter to glean what I could. Legumes and pulses opened my eyes to the possibilities of making traditional cooking work for us with our meager finances.

Cooking a big pot of beans and then turning them into several meals, while flavoring each meal a bit differently to reduce boredom, was the answer to improving our diet.

Because we concentrated our food dollars on budget-friendly beans, broth, and whole grains—and stopped buying almost all processed foods—we were soon able to squeak out enough funds to add in a small number of things like healthy fats, grass-fed beef, and raw milk.

Within only a few weeks of our new traditional foods and Stretchy Beans way of eating, we all noticed a decrease in our stomach issues. I was excited to discover my clothes were fitting differently. That first year I lost 20 pounds without effort.

While I am sharing links to recipes here, I should tell you that many times I don't use a recipe when putting our meals together. I create the dishes while standing at the stove. I have several Basic Formulas that I use for common dishes, which I share in my book *Design a Dish*. I find that formula cooking is one of the best ways to make the most of our food budget.

How to Use This Book

This book is designed to be a guide to help you stretch your food dollars with beans and legumes. I've added sections for beans that are widely available. There are many regional or home-raised beans that are similar to the beans I list. Feel free to use those instead. I included recipes where it's suitable, but many of the instructions are very loose and more of a method as opposed to strict instructions.

While many of the recipes do include meat in some form, I list this as optional (but recommended). If you can't fit meat into your budget, leave it out. The dish will still be delicious!

Nutrition

Beans and legumes are high in protein. A half cup of beans provides 7 grams of protein, the equivalent of 1 ounce of meat.

In addition to protein, beans provide minerals—including magnesium, potassium, phosphorus, iron, and molybdenum—as well as B vitamins such as folate and thiamine. Folate, also known as vitamin B9, is needed to make red and white blood cells in bone marrow, convert carbohydrates into energy, produce DNA and RNA, decreases risk of congenital deformities, can help with depression, and much more.

Beans and legumes also provide both omega-3 and omega-6 fatty acids.

Beans for Food Storage and Preparedness

Beans and legumes are also an important part of our pantry building/food storage plan. When stored properly, they keep wonderfully!

We buy our beans in bulk, 25- to 50-pound bags, usually through Azure Standard or special ordering via a local grocery store. The beans arrive in paper bags, but these bags are not suitable for long-term storage (neither are plastic bags), so we repackage them.

To store beans for long-term use, we use 5-gallon buckets with lids (collected from local bakeries for free to $1 per bucket), mylar bags, and oxygen absorbers.

We recently opened up a bucket of beans after four years, and they were still fresh and perfect. I have a friend who stored lentils in this manner before Y2K. She used her last bucket in 2013, and it was as fresh as the first bucket.

You can also order beans already packaged in buckets or in #10 cans from places like Augason Farms. This is a good option if you prefer to not do it yourself. I've found the prices to be higher using this option, but it's easy. And, under the appropriate conditions, the shelf life of the #10 cans is up to 30 years!

Many people avoid beans in their food storage plan due to the amount of water and fuel needed to make them edible. While the water issue is outside the scope of this book, I do address alternative preparation methods. These are methods I use in my everyday kitchen, so I know they work!

Broth

"Then Gideon went in and prepared a young goat and unleavened bread from an ephah of flour; he put the meat in a basket and the broth in a pot, and brought them out to him under the oak and presented them." Judges 6:19

Broth is a healing tradition that has been around for centuries. Grandma's chicken soup—made from real chicken bones and *not* those little cubes—doesn't just taste good, it also includes healing properties.

So simple! Making broth is one of the easiest, and least expensive, additions you can make to your real food kitchen. Purchasing a whole chicken to enjoy, as not just the roasted meat but also with the bones as broth, is an economical and straightforward option. If you order a whole or half of a beef, be sure to ask for the bones. You may also be able to find bones at your local health-food store.

And when money is really tight, save every bone that enters your home.

According to the Weston A. Price Foundation's article "Broth is Beautiful," broth contains minerals in a form the body can absorb easily—not just calcium but also magnesium, phosphorus, silicon, sulfur, and trace minerals. It contains the broken-down material from cartilage and tendons—stuff like chondroitin sulphates and glucosamine, now sold as expensive supplements for arthritis and joint pain.

Have you cooked a whole chicken and then put the remains in the fridge? When you come back to it, did it have a thick gel coating? You've made gelatin! This natural gelatin, formed by the collagen in the meat and bones, is rich in protein. But even though it's rich in protein, it lacks essential amino acids, making it an incomplete protein. While not a complete protein on its own, broth acts as a protein sparer, which allows even a small amount of meat to stretch into a complete meal.

Because of the wonderful, and inexpensive, nutrition broth provides, my Stretchy Beans method almost always includes the use of either meat broth or bone broth when cooking the beans or finishing the recipes.

Meat Broth vs Bone Broth

In many ways, the use of meat broth and bone broth are interchangeable. For the purpose of this book, I'll break down the main differences and how each will play a part in your Stretchy Bean methods.

Meat broth is made from simmering meat—which may contain bones and/or vegetables but doesn't have to—for a short amount of time. Just long enough to cook the meat.

Bone broth uses animal bones, which may still have bits of meat attached; a splash of apple cider vinegar, which helps draw out the minerals; and often includes vegetables, which can be fresh or from scraps. It then cooks for an extended length of time—24 to 48 hours, or possibly longer—to leach all the wonderful minerals out of the bones.

To get the most bang for your food buck, my method utilizes both meat broth and bone broth.

Meat broth is easily made when cooking a chicken or roast on the stovetop, in the crockpot, or in the Instant Pot. The liquid that accumulates while the meat cooks is an easy meat broth.

After picking all the meat off the chicken or roast, the leftover bones become the basis for bone broth, making this an almost free food! Not only do I utilize these "fresh" bones, I've been known to save every bone that enters my house. If we enjoy roasted chicken drumsticks for dinner, I'll collect everyone's chicken bones, rinse them off, and then store them in the freezer until I have enough to make a batch of broth. Same thing with fish bones, shrimp shells, and the bones of any other item you might enjoy.

Yes, some people might have issues with the ewww factor, but if you're really watching your pennies, this is a great way to find extra nutrition and flavor from something that would otherwise end up in the garbage.

Making Meat Broth

Meat broth is so easy to make. I essentially gave you the simple instructions in my introduction paragraph above, but keep reading if you'd like a few more details.

I often make meat broth when braising tough stew meats. These tough meats, cooked simply in water with a little salt, can then be used in a quickly prepared dish with whatever seasonings you desire.

Simmer the meat until it's cooked through and tender. Depending on the size of the cut, this can take several hours. Strain the meat from the broth. (See Bonus Nutrition Tips below.) The accumulated broth should be put in a jar and stored in the refrigerator. The next day, check the broth for fat and skim it off. Use this fat for your cooking needs. The broth is now ready to use.

A whole chicken cooked on the stovetop, in the crockpot, or in the pressure cooker makes wonderful meat broth. My preference is to use my crockpot because it's an almost-hands-off method.

Sprinkle the chicken with salt, add 1 cup of water, and cook on low until the meat is falling off the bone, about 8 hours. Remove the chicken and set aside to cool. The accumulated broth should be stored in the refrigerator in mason jars. Pick the meat from the bones and use the bones for bone broth. (See Bonus Nutrition Tips below.) The next day, check the broth for fat and skim it off. Use this fat for your cooking needs.

In addition, you can make meat broth from any meat pieces, meaty bones, or necks from any animal: beef, wild game, chicken, turkey, duck, rabbit, pork, lamb, even fish. Simply cook until the meat is falling off the bone. Remove solids (see Bonus Nutrition Tips below) and refrigerate the broth. The next day, check the broth for fat and skim it off. Use this fat for your cooking needs and use any meat for your meals.

What's this about fish? Yes! We often poach trout until it flakes and then use the flaked trout in a fish chowder. You can use any fish for poaching and then keep the meat broth, but for bone broth you'll only want to use non-oily fish. I find fish broth a little strong for using as my Stretchy Beans broth, but it's a nutritional powerhouse that's excellent for giving an exotic flair to your dishes.

Bonus Nutrition Tips!

When you are really trying to stretch your food dollars, you need to get the most nutrition possible for the best value. Here's a great way to add extra gut-healing properties to your broth.

Remove all the soft tissues and bits from the bones as best as you can. These soft bits are basically anything "soft" that could be blended, i.e., skin, ligaments, cartilage, etc. Take care that you do not include any pieces of bone or hard pieces. This changes the texture, making it quite unpleasant. Blend up these soft pieces and save them to add back to any soup, stew, or chili.

Making Bone Broth

Bone broth is made from bones that may have a small amount of meat still attached. I used to add vegetables to my broth, but I no longer do so. With the long cooking time, the vegetables can give the broth a bitter taste. Bone broth can be cooked on the stovetop, in the crockpot, or in a pressure cooker. The key is a long, slow cook to get as much nutrition out of the bones as possible. Breaking open the bones before cooking will increase this nutrient release.

Get creative with finding bones! One thing I do is put the word out to farmers and ranchers, letting them know I'd be happy to take carcasses and chicken feet (these make the best broth!) off their hands. Many will sell these at an incredible price. Some health-food stores also sell bones.

And I save bones from cooked meals to use too. If I have a bone-in roast of some sort, it is fair game for broth. If it's a small bone, it goes in the freezer until I have enough for a pot. You can separate by species or keep them all together, either way works.

To make a batch of bone broth, you should have the equivalent of bones to equal one whole chicken or somewhere there about—a dozen drumsticks or several bones from steak, chops, roast, etc. Just use your best judgment on how much you need. It doesn't have to be exact.

For the stovetop or crockpot, put the bones in the container and fill it almost full with water. Add a couple tablespoons of apple cider vinegar. Don't worry! Your broth won't have a strong vinegar taste. The ACV will help draw out the nutrients.

On the stovetop, simmer for:

- Fish: 6 to 8 hours
- Chicken: 18 to 24 hours (after a couple hours, I like to pick off any meat on the bones to use in other recipes)
- Beef, lamb, game, pork: 36 hours (after a couple hours, I like to pick off any meat on the bones to use in other recipes)
- Crustacean shells (shrimp, crab, lobster, crayfish, etc.): 4 to 6 hours

In the crockpot, cook on low for:

- Fish: 6 to 8 hours
- Chicken: 18 to 24 hours (after a couple hours, I like to pick off any meat on the bones to use in other recipes)
- Beef, lamb, game, pork: 36 hours (after a couple hours, I like to pick off any meat on the bones to use in other recipes)
- Crustacean shells (shrimp, crab, lobster, crayfish, etc.): 4 to 6 hours

In the pressure cooker (I have not done fish or shells in this manner):

- Chicken, beef, lamb, game, pork: 2 hours and then natural pressure release

After the cooking time is complete, strain the bones by putting a big bowl underneath a colander. Then strain again with a smaller colander if needed. Store the broth in mason jars.

After chilling, any fat that accumulates on the top of the broth should be discarded. Because of the extended cooking time, this fat may become rancid and have an unpleasant taste.

Follow the Bonus Nutrition Tips from the Making Meat Broth section above, removing all the soft tissues and bits from the bones as best as you can.

After the soft bits have been removed, put the bones back in for a second batch and repeat the process.

Repeat for a third batch of broth, adding a couple more tablespoons of vinegar.

Note: For fish or shells, I only do one batch.

Perpetual Broth

Perpetual broth is a great way to always have healthy bone broth on hand and ready to go. This can be made in a crockpot or on the stovetop.

Put the bones in a crockpot or large stockpot and cover with water. Add a tablespoon or so of apple cider vinegar.

If you're using the stovetop, bring to a boil for about 1 hour, then simmer on low to medium heat.

For the crockpot, cook on high for 1 hour and then turn it to low.

After 12 to 24 hours, ladle out the broth you need or fill up a mason jar (or two) and move to the fridge. Be sure to leave at least a quart of broth behind. At this point, you can follow the Bonus Nutrition Tips from the Making Meat Broth section, removing all the soft tissues and bits from the bones as best as you can. Once you've removed the soft bits, refill the crockpot or stockpot with water and follow the cooking instructions again.

Twelve to 24 hours later, ladle out the broth you need or fill up another mason jar (or two) and move to the fridge.

Repeat daily for 5 days, then clean out the pot and start over again.

Vegetable Broth

Vegetable broth is a lot quicker to make than bone broth and is a good way to use up scrap veggies. Like the miscellaneous bones, keep a container of veggie scraps in your freezer: onion ends/skins, celery ends, and carrots peels/ends. Just about any vegetable will work.

Put everything in a stockpot and cover with water. If you have washed eggshells, add these too! Bring to a rolling boil for 10 minutes. Skim as needed, then lower to a simmer and cook for 2 hours. Strain out veggies and eggshells by placing a colander in a large bowl. Store in mason jars.

I've done this many times when money and broth bones were in short supply. It works great!

Note: This can be made in the Instant Pot as well. Cook on high pressure for 20 minutes in the sealed position.

Healthy Fats

A quick note about fat. For years, butter and lard were demonized while industrial fats and oils were promoted as heart healthy. Good fats, bad fats, it can all be very confusing. I came of age during a time when fat was the enemy. I strived for a diet low in fat. When I did "need" to add fat to my diet, I used canola or vegetable oil since they were "approved" fats. When I first started researching traditional diets, the idea of adding animal fat to my diet was scary. Very scary.

But the more I researched, the more I was convinced a low-fat diet wasn't the best for my health. And it most certainly wasn't best for the health of my children. Mother's milk provides a higher proportion of cholesterol than almost any other food. It also contains over 50 percent of its calories as fat—much of it being saturated fat. Both cholesterol and saturated fat are essential for growth in babies and children, especially the development of the brain. Fats are vital to brain development and energy, and they also provide a role in the formation of hormones. However, the fats we eat must be chosen with care.

We lean toward animal fats such as lard, tallow, schmaltz (chicken fat), and duck fat; tropical fats such as coconut oil and palm oil; and plant fats like olive and avocado oil. In small quantities, we also use sesame oil and flax oil. "The Skinny on Fats" by the Weston A. Price Foundation has excellent information on fats' bad rap.

In my recipes, you'll often see "healthy fat." When cooking, you want a fat that can handle the heat. Lard, tallow, ghee (clarified butter), and schmaltz are excellent options.

Finding locally raised pastured animals is the least expensive option for animal fats. When we order a half pig, I ask for the fat. When we process our chickens or ducks, I save the fat. When I had a cow share for raw milk, I was also able to get homemade ghee. In the Broth chapter, I shared how I skim the fat off of the broth and save this to use. Please also notice when I mention not to save the fat on the broth; prolonged cooking of the broth can cause the fat to become rancid.

Coconut oil is another fat for cooking (not recommended for deep frying). If the idea of imparting a coconut flavor to your savory dishes holds little appeal, choose an expeller-pressed coconut oil. It's less expensive than virgin coconut oil and goes through a steam deodorizing process, resulting in a very bland taste. Virgin coconut oil, which retains the odor and taste of fresh coconuts, is great in baked good or for making coconut candy, but it's not as great when cooking beans. I order my expeller-pressed coconut oil online, 5 gallons at a time. The largest part of our food budget goes to insuring we have an abundance of healthy fats available.

For gentle sautéing over low heat, I'll use butter or a combination of butter and olive oil. Neither butter nor olive oil are suitable for frying or cooking over high heat. A good-quality extra-virgin olive oil is really best kept unheated and used in salads or drizzled over hummus. And butter should, of course, be spread liberally on your homemade bread.

Some people cook using avocado oil. It is extremely heat stable and able to withstand high temperatures. I do love avocado oil, but the cost makes it more of a luxury item. When I can fit it in my budget, I'll buy it to use in salad dressing and homemade mayonnaise.

The addition of whole foods—such as avocado, whole-fat cheese, whole-fat (raw) milk, cream, whole-fat yogurt, sour cream, egg yolk, fatty fish (such as salmon), pastured meats, and other unprocessed, naturally fatty foods—are also recommended. Beans are naturally low in fat, so the addition of these items, even in small quantities, will be helpful.

Spices and Other Flavorings

I use a variety of herbs and spices in my Stretchy Bean recipes and methods. When cooking beans, it's best to not add salt until the end of the cooking process to help keep the beans tender. Once the beans are cooked, spice away! Some of my dishes will specify seasoning simply with only sea salt and pepper, then adding additional flavoring—such as hot sauce—at the table. Some of the dishes are well flavored with curry powder, chili powder, garlic powder, and more. Adding a variety of dried herbs and spices to your pantry will be a benefit.

When stored properly, ground spices and herbs have a storage life of two to three years. Dried whole spices and herbs have a slightly longer storage life of three to five years with proper storage. Spices should be stored in a cool, dark place. If you purchase your spices in bulk, you can preserve them in mason jars or vacuum sealed bags to help maintain their flavor and freshness longer.

In addition to spices, I like to keep a selection of vinegars, soy sauce (or tamari), Worcestershire sauce, and a few other miscellaneous items. These flavorings can really "spice" up a dish and take beans from ordinary to extraordinary.

Items I Keep on Hand Include the Following:

- Sea salt (I keep a couple of varieties, but for everyday use I prefer Redmond Real Salt)
- Ground black pepper
- Whole black peppercorns

- Dry mustard
- Dried thyme
- Dried dill
- Dried basil
- Ground ginger
- Marjoram
- Ground cinnamon
- Chili powder
- Cayenne pepper
- Ground cumin
- Garlic powder
- Granulated garlic (this is great to use in slow cooking dishes like soups and stews)
- Dried minced onion
- Paprika, sweet
- Smoked paprika
- Dried oregano
- Dried parsley
- Ground turmeric
- Ground cardamom
- Ground clove
- Garam Masala
- Ground curry powder
- Apple cider vinegar, raw
- Rice wine vinegar
- Red wine vinegar
- White wine vinegar
- Balsamic vinegar
- Worcestershire sauce
- Lemon juice
- Lime juice

Cooking Beans

Soak First

We all know beans have a bit of a—*ahem*—reputation. With proper preparation, we can help eliminate the digestive issues associated with beans.

A quick internet search will produce many recipes that allow you to skip the soaking process or do a "quick" soak. I don't recommend this. Without a proper long-term soak, our healthy beans are likely to produce gas and discomfort.

In addition, beans contain phytic acid, like all seeds do, which may impede mineral absorption. We can neutralize this by soaking. Harder beans (such as pinto, kidney, black, navy beans, etc.) contain large, complex sugars called oligosaccharides that can "completely confound digestion."

By giving our beans a good, long soak in an ample amount of water, we can help with the digestive and mineral absorption issues.

How to Soak Beans

Sort your beans to remove any debris.

Put in a colander and rinse.

Move the beans to a bowl or cooking container and cover with enough water to go over the beans by a couple of inches. Ideally, you should use warm water to help with the soaking process. Admittedly, I don't. I use room temperature water straight from the Berkey filter, choosing to extend the soaking time up to 24 hours. If you choose to soak for this length of time, you should change the water at least once. An overnight soak in warmish water is suitable for most people and most beans.

If you are particularly sensitive to beans, and have known digestive issues even with soaking, you should choose a 24-hour soak. Also, consider sprouting your beans for several days before cooking.

At the end of your soaking time, there may be some scum or bubbles. Drain and rinse your beans. They should smell fresh. If they smell sour or rotten, rinse them some more. If they still smell bad, there may have been an issue with the beans and they should be discarded. This is rare, but it could happen.

How to Cook Beans

When cooking beans, my goal is to make one large pot to use for three or four meals during the week. This helps cuts down on my food costs and also the time I spend in the kitchen each day.

I usually soak 5 cups of beans at a time (approximately 2 pounds, depending on type of bean), which seems to be a good amount for a family of five, providing three meals and often leftovers for lunch.

There are numerous ways to cook beans—and all require little effort!

Note: With all of the following cooking methods, you should salt your beans after they're cooked to prevent them from becoming too tough.

Stovetop

Start with 5 cups of picked-over beans (to remove any stones or debris) and rinse thoroughly.

Soak the beans in plain water the night before you want to cook them, or up to 24 hours (be sure to change the water at least one time if soaking for a full day). I usually soak them right in the stockpot I'll use to cook them in, making sure I've added plenty of water. The beans will swell and nearly triple in volume.

At the end of your soaking time, drain the soaking water off, giving them a good rinse, and put the beans back in the stockpot.

Cover the beans with homemade broth, water, or a mixture of both. I prefer to cook my beans in bone broth to add more nutrients. If I don't have any broth made, I'll often add a package of previously cooked bones from my freezer stash and then cover it all with water.

Bring the pot of beans to a boil and then cover and simmer for 1 to 1 ½ hours; longer as needed or less for smaller legumes like lentils. When finished cooking, season with salt, pepper, and garlic.

The beans are now ready to be divided up. Take out enough beans for supper, then divide the remaining beans into two or three other portions, depending on your menu plan for the week.

Crockpot

Start with 5 cups of picked-over beans (to remove any stones or debris) and rinse thoroughly.

In the crockpot, soak the beans in plain water the night before you want to cook them (or up to 24 hours, changing the water at least one time).

The next morning, drain the soaking water off and put the beans back in the crockpot, then cover with homemade broth, water, or a mixture of both.

Cook on low for 5 to 8 hours. Larger beans take longer than smaller beans. When they're thoroughly cooked, lightly season the entire pot with salt, pepper, and garlic.

Take out enough beans for supper, then divide the remaining beans into two or three other portions, depending on your menu plan for the week.

Instant Pot or Pressure Cooker

Start with 5 cups of picked-over beans (to remove any stones or debris) and rinsed thoroughly.

In the Instant Pot or pressure cooker, soak the beans in plain water the night before you want to cook them (or up to 24 hours, changing the water at least one time).

The next morning, drain the soaking water off and put the beans back in the Instant Pot, then cover with homemade broth, water, or a mixture of both.

Cooking times vary based on the type of pressure cooker and the type of beans you use. Follow the instructions in your Instant Pot manual or pressure cooker, or look up cooking times online. Please be aware, beans that have been soaked will cook faster than beans that were not soaked. I've found 11 minutes with a natural release to work well for pinto beans. Your experience may vary based on the age of your beans and your altitude.

When they're thoroughly cooked, lightly season the entire pot with salt, pepper, and garlic.

Take out enough beans for supper, then divide the remaining beans into two or three other portions, depending on your menu plan for the week.

Note: I don't use the Instant Pot very often, but my friend Wardee at Traditional Cooking School is a pro with it. If you're new to pressure cooking, she has two pressure cooking courses that are very affordable and will teach you everything you need to know.

Alternative, Energy-Saving Cooking Methods

Woodstove

Beans turn out wonderfully on the woodstove!

Soak the beans for your chosen soaking time, pour off the soaking water, and give them a good rinse. Add broth, water, or a mixture of both and then bring it to a boil on the stovetop.

Move your pot to the woodstove and cook until finished. It takes 8 to 10 hours to cook beans like black and pinto. Lentils cook in just over an hour. Of course, these cooking times can be faster or slower depending on how hot your fire is.

Hay Box

Another cheap cooking method is a hay box cooker, or some variation thereof. This is something like a nonelectric crockpot. The idea here is to heat a dish to boiling and then nestle it inside of an insulated box.

You can buy a Wonderbag, make your own hay box cooker, or do what I do—use an old cooler and some towels. This works great! You still need to use your stovetop to start the process, but the cooking time is limited.

First, in a pot that will fit inside your hay box, soak your beans overnight and then drain and rinse in the morning. Return the beans to the pot and cover with broth, water, or a mixture of both.

On the stovetop, boil for 10 minutes and then move the pot to your hay box cooker. Depending on the variety of bean, it can take anywhere from 8 to 12 hours for them to soften.

If you choose the old cooler and towel method, you may wish to add a couple jars of hot, almost-boiling water. My cooler isn't as efficient as it once was, so the jars of hot water help with holding in the heat.

Solar Oven

When conditions are right, I may also use my Sun Oven. The Sun Oven is amazing! But as much as I love it, I admit, I don't use it often enough. While we have plenty of sun and it heats up wonderfully, the wind can sometimes be an issue. And let me tell you, we have some wind in Wyoming!

But seriously, the Sun Oven works great and makes those inexpensive beans even more economical by not adding the additional cost of electricity. Plus, it's so simple to use.

After soaking and rinsing your beans, just fill the pot with broth or water, or a mixture of both, put it in the Sun Oven, and let it cook. The length of cooking time may vary depending on the temperature you are able to achieve. This is not a "set it and forget it" method. You'll need to monitor the progress and adjust the oven to best capture the sunshine.

Sprouting Beans

Instead of cooking the beans, you can skip it all together! Not that I'm suggesting gnawing on those dry beans and breaking a tooth—a visit to the dentist would definitely negate the cost savings of having beans and legumes in your diet.

We're talking sprouts!

While this does work for almost any variety of beans, I especially love sprouting lentils and garbanzo beans. Sprouting takes a few days, so you'll need to plan ahead.

What do you do with these lovely sprouted beans?

So, so much!

Lentils that have sprouted at least two days (just a small tail) are perfect for tacos. Once they've sprouted a few days and have a longer tail, they are excellent as the main component of a salad or made into sprouted lentil burgers. So good! My mouth is almost watering just thinking about those delicious burgers.

Sprouted and lightly steamed garbanzo beans also make a wonderful patty, and lightly mashed garbanzos are amazing as a taco filling. And, of course, I'd be remiss to not mention hummus (just substitute the cooked beans with sprouted and steamed beans). I may be guilty of skipping the chips and eating this with a spoon! Sprouted pinto or black beans also make a wonderful, hummus-like dip.

Any sprouted bean makes a nice addition to a salad. We do a lot of main dish salads in the summer, and adding sprouted beans gives it an amazing punch and extra nutrition.

The cooking and sprouting method below works well for just about every bean or legume—except kidney beans. We do not sprout kidney beans. More on why in the kidney bean section.

How to Sprout

There are many ways to sprout. You can buy fancy sprouting equipment or jars with special lids. But I'm all about economy and shortcuts. My favorite method for sprouting legumes is to use a bowl and a colander—two items that are already in most kitchens. And because I sprout a large amount of beans at one time, the bowl and colander are a better size than many other options.

Start with 5 cups of picked-over beans (to remove any stones or debris) and rinse thoroughly.

Soak the beans in plain water the night before you want to sprout them or up to 24 hours (be sure to rinse and replace the water at least one time if you're doing a long soak). Put them in a big bowl, stockpot, or other container. Make sure you've added plenty of water because the beans will swell and nearly triple in volume.

In the morning, drain the beans into a colander and rinse thoroughly. Give the colander a good shake to remove as much water as possible. Set a plate or similar dish on the counter, then place the colander on the dish and cover with a towel. Your beans may drain a little more, but the plate should prevent a mess. The towel will keep dust off of the beans.

Rinse every 12 hours for 3 to 5 days. After they have sprouted and have tails, give them a final rinse. Drain and shake to remove as much water as possible and then store in the fridge until ready to use. They can be rinsed every two days to keep fresh.

While the 3 to 5 day sprouting method is perfect for producing a nice, long tail, I tend to use my beans in various stages of sprouting. You'll read more about this in the individual bean and legume sections.

Baked Beans

This is a fun option! Make a big batch of baked beans and turn it into Stretchy Beans. You'll want to use a heartier bean—something in the pinto or white bean family is nice. But black beans or kidney beans will also work. Kidney beans will result in dish with a slightly different texture.

Baked Beans in the Oven

These amazing baked beans far surpass anything out of a can. This is a recipe adapted from *The Complete Tightwad Gazette*.

Not-Really Maine Baked Beans

- 2 ½ pounds dried beans (about 5 cups)
- 1 teaspoon baking soda
- 2 medium onions, diced
- ½ pound bacon, turkey bacon, farmer's bacon, sausage, or ground meat (optional)
- ¼ cup honey
- ⅔ cup molasses
- 2 teaspoons dry mustard
- ½ teaspoon sea salt

Pick over the beans to remove any stones or debris and rinse thoroughly.

Soak the beans in plain water the night before you want to cook them or up to 24 hours. I usually soak them right in the stockpot I'll use to cook them in, making sure I've added plenty of water. The beans will swell and nearly triple in volume.

At the end of your soaking time, drain the soaking water off, give them a good rinse, and put the beans back in the stockpot and cover with fresh water. Add the baking soda, then parboil the beans until the skins crack when blown upon.

If you are using sausage or ground meat, you'll want to brown it when the beans are close to done.

You'll need 2 bean pots or large casserole dishes for baking the beans. Cut the onions in a large dice and mix in with the beans. Divide the parboiled beans between the two dishes, reserving a quart of water.

If using bacon or farmer's bacon (uncured), cut and add to the top of the beans. If using sausage, add the browned sausage now.

In a separate bowl, mix honey, molasses, dry mustard, and salt with the quart of reserved bean water. Mix well to combine and then divide between the two dishes. Bake at 300 degrees for 6 to 8 hours. You may need to add additional water during baking.

Baked Beans in the Crockpot

Making baked beans in the crockpot is similar to cooking regular beans, just with a few additions to give it the baked bean flavor. I like to use the recipe for Not-Really Maine Baked Beans (See Baked Beans in the Oven Recipe).

Start with 5 cups of picked-over beans to remove any stones or debris and rinse thoroughly.

In the crockpot, soak the beans in plain water the night before you want to cook them (or up to 24 hours, changing the water at least one time).

The next morning, drain the soaking water and give them a good rinse. Before putting the beans back in the crockpot, roughly dice two onions and add to the bottom. Cover with the drained beans. Add browned sausage/meat or cut-up raw bacon (optional).

In a separate bowl, mix honey, molasses, dry mustard, and salt with 4 cups of fresh water. Mix well to combine and then pour over the beans. Cook on low for at least 8 hours.

Baked Beans on the Stovetop

When making baked beans on the stovetop, I use the same barbeque sauce as I do for my Short Rib recipe.

- 1 cup ketchup (HFCS free) or tomato sauce
- ¼ cup tamari or naturally fermented soy sauce
- 2 tablespoons olive oil
- 2 tablespoons honey (or ¼ cup Sucanat or another natural sweetener)
- 2 tablespoons molasses (optional)
- ½ teaspoon sea salt
- ¼ teaspoon black pepper
- 1 teaspoon garlic powder (or 3 cloves fresh garlic, minced)
- 1 cup water or broth
- ¼ cup dried onion (or ½ cup fresh onion, minced)
- 4 or 5 cups cooked beans (depending on how many people you are serving and how saucy you want the dish)
- ½ to 2 cups precooked meat (optional)

Combine the tomato sauce, soy sauce, olive oil, sweetener, molasses, salt, pepper, garlic, broth, and onion in a stew pot. Mix well and bring to a boil.

Turn down the heat and simmer for 5 to 10 minutes to blend the flavors and soften the onion. Add beans and meat (if using), then heat through.

Meal Options 1

- Baked Beans
- Corn Pone
- Dunkin' Soup

When we're tired of eating boiled beans, baking gives them new life. The slow all-day simmer, perfect for a cold winter's day, fills the house with warmth and makes my mouth water. By using the crockpot or stovetop recipe, you can make "baked" beans a warm-weather treat also.

To make the most of our meals, I like to divide out future servings before the Day 1 meal. For Day 1, the baked beans are the main dish. Then you'll need 3 cups of baked beans for Day 2 and 2 cups of baked beans for Day 3. Any leftovers can be frozen in 1 or 2 cup containers for future meals.

Day 1

Baked Beans

Simply serve baked beans, salad (or other vegetable), and homemade bread. Refer to the cooking options and recipes listed previously for making baked beans.

Day 2

Corn Pone

This is another *Tightwad Gazette* recipe, with slight alterations. I'm not sure if this is *actually* Corn Pone, but we'll just go with it.

- ¼ to ½ pound ground meat (optional but recommended)
- ½ onion, diced
- 1 tablespoon healthy fat, for sautéing
- 1 teaspoon sea salt, divided
- 1 teaspoon Worcestershire sauce
- 1 can diced tomatoes
- 3 cups baked beans
- 1 cup cornmeal
- 1 cup flour (your choice; I like whole wheat)
- 2 teaspoons baking powder
- 1 egg
- 1 cup milk
- ¼ cup melted butter, coconut oil, or mild olive oil

Preheat oven to 425 degrees.

Brown the ground meat (hamburger, wild game, pork, chicken, etc.) with the onion and healthy fat. When the meat is brown and the onion is soft, combine with ½ teaspoon sea salt, Worcestershire sauce, diced tomatoes, and baked beans in a large casserole dish or cast iron frying pan.

In a separate bowl, make cornbread batter by combining cornmeal, flour, baking powder, and ½ teaspoon of sea salt. Mix well. Add egg, milk, and melted butter or oil. Combine until just mixed.

Top the meat and bean mixture with a layer of cornbread batter about ½ inch thick. I usually just plop the batter on and then smooth it out with a rubber spatula.

Bake for 25 to 30 minutes until the cornbread is golden and everything underneath is bubbly.

Day 3

Dunkin' Soup

This recipe is also from *The Tightwad Gazette*.

- 2 cups baked beans
- 1 can stewed tomatoes
- 1 celery stalk with leaves
- 1 onion, finely diced
- Sea salt, to taste
- Black pepper, to taste

Put all ingredients in a cooking pot and puree with an immersion blender, or puree in a standard blender and then move to a cooking pot. Heat to boiling, then allow to simmer for 15 minutes, stirring often.

This soup gets its name from the tradition of eating it by dipping—or dunkin'—bread into the soup. It's also delicious when eaten with a spoon.

Meal Options 2

- Baked Beans
- Breakfast for Dinner: Baked Beans Over Pancakes
- Bean Chowder

This rotation takes me back to my childhood and my great-grandma Lydia's pancakes topped with a scoop of beans. Baked beans over the top of sourdough (or your favorite) pancakes sounds strange, but it tastes delicious. The smokey sweetness of the beans is a wonderful stand-in for syrup. The combination of the whole grain with the bean makes a complete protein, providing much more nourishment than the standard way of eating pancakes. If you'd like, top it all with a fried or poached egg. Yum!

For Day 1, the baked beans are the main dish. Then you'll need 2 cups of baked beans for Day 2, and 3 cups of baked beans for Day 3. Any leftovers can be frozen in 1 or 2 cup containers for future meals.

Day 1

Baked Beans

A meal on their own! Simply serve baked beans, salad (or other vegetable), and homemade bread.

Day 2

Breakfast for Dinner: Baked Beans Over Pancakes

Make your favorite pancakes (we like sourdough or buttermilk). I like to keep these fairly small. Not as small as silver dollar size but not serving platter size either; maybe 4 inches across.

While cooking the pancakes, heat the baked beans. You may need to add a little water so the beans are a thinner consistency—not thin like syrup, but thin enough to run over the pancake. Poach (or fry) one or two eggs per person.

Put the pancake on the plate, top it with a ladle of baked beans, then perch the egg on top.

Feel free to keep the items separate if your child, like mine, prefers food in its individual spaces.

Day 3

Bean Chowder

Adapted from...you guessed it: *The Tightwad Gazette.*

- 6 slices bacon (cut up) or ¼ to ½ pound sausage or ground meat (optional, but recommended)
- 1 onion, chopped
- 2 tablespoons flour
- 3 cups broth
- 2 medium potatoes, peeled and diced
- ¼ teaspoon dried thyme, crushed
- 1 teaspoon sea salt
- Black pepper, to taste (less than ¼ teaspoon)
- 3 cups baked beans
- 1 cup heavy cream or sour cream
- Fresh parsley (optional)

In a saucepan, cook the meat with onion until the meat is done and the onion is tender.

Blend in flour. Slowly add broth, cooking and stirring to prevent clumps, until bubbly. Add diced potatoes, thyme, sea salt, and pepper. Cover and simmer 12 to 15 minutes or until the potatoes are soft.

Stir in the beans and heat through. When everything is warm, add the heavy cream or sour cream and stir to blend. Top individual bowls with parsley and additional sour cream, if desired.

Pinto Beans

Pintos have been a familiar food for me since I was a child. My mama would make a big pot of pintos and a pan of cornbread every Friday night. Over the weekend, we'd eat bowl after bowl of beans.

My Stretchy Pinto Beans are like the way my mama served beans, except after the first night of plain beans, I like to create slightly different dishes than just serving beans by the bowl. Be sure to refer to the Cooking Beans section for options on how to cook pinto beans.

While this section is for pinto beans, feel free to substitute with other beans. And although meat is listed as an optional ingredient, all these recipes can be made meat-free since beans combined with grains create a complete protein.

Keep in mind, these meal options are only a suggestion based on what I've done and what works for me. Use this as a guide only and find what works best for you. And be sure to check other bean types for additional ideas. The options are limitless!

Meal Options 1

- Pinto Beans and Rice
- Bean, Cheese, and Rice Burritos
- Layered Tortilla Pie

Have you read *The Long Winter*? It's one of the Little House books by Laura Ingalls Wilder. In the story, Ma starts a pot of beans on the woodstove early in the morning. For their noon meal, they have the thin broth that has accumulated during the cooking process. Then they have the cooked beans for supper. When I think of my Stretchy Bean dishes, especially the pinto beans, Ma's bean broth makes me smile. While this isn't a method that I've employed in my Stretchy Bean meals, it's a definite option and one that should be considered when the food budget is tight. If you do have bean broth for lunch, add a little extra water to finish the cooking process.

For Day 1, the pinto beans are the main dish. Then you'll need 3 cups of beans for Day 2, and 4 cups of beans for Day 3. I like to take out the amount I'll need for future days before serving the Day 1 meal. Any leftover beans can be frozen in 1-cup containers for later use or served for lunches during the week. I also make a double batch of rice so I have enough for both Day 1 and Day 2.

Day 1

Pinto Beans and Rice

Make a simple meal of beans and rice served with sautéed cabbage and onions (or other vegetable or salad of choice).

I season the beans simply with salt and pepper and then serve them over rice. Family members can then add additional seasoning at the table. My husband likes to add hot sauce to his. My mom used to put apple cider vinegar and a sprinkle of sugar over her beans, so that's often what I do; it's kind of a sweet and sour experience.

Day 2

Bean, Cheese, and Rice Burritos

These are so easy you that don't really need a recipe!

- ¼ to 1 pound ground meat (optional; can be beef, wild game, chicken, pork, etc.)
- ½ onion, finely minced
- Healthy fat
- ¼ teaspoon garlic powder
- ½ to 1 teaspoon chili powder, to taste
- ½ teaspoon paprika (optional, but recommended)
- ½ teaspoon ground cumin
- ¼ teaspoon dried oregano
- ½ teaspoon sea salt (plus additional to taste)
- Black pepper, to taste
- 3 cups cooked beans
- 2 to 3 cups leftover rice, warmed separately
- Shredded cheese (your choice of variety and amount)
- Toppers such as sour cream, jalapeno peppers, minced onion, salsa, cilantro, etc. (optional)
- Tortillas

If using ground meat, brown it with onion and healthy fat and then break the meat into very small pieces. You want pebbles, not chunks. I use a fork to achieve this tiny consistency. If omitting the meat, lightly sauté the onion in fat until translucent.

When the meat (if using) and onion are ready, add the spices and stir. Then add the beans, stirring around to gather the fat and spices.

As it warms, use a potato masher to mash the beans; you may need to add a little extra fat or water during this process. You want some of the beans mashed and some left whole (not a smooth puree). Taste it. What does it need? Adjust your seasonings to suit.

When the beans are warm and delicious, everyone is ready to make their burrito. Add the beans, then rice, then cheese, and any toppers. Wrap it up and enjoy!

Note: I like to make my own tortillas. We love the sourdough tortillas from Traditional Cooking School, but you can use your favorite recipe for flour tortillas or use store-bought ones. Make a double batch (or purchase enough) so you have tortillas for Day 3.

Day 3

Layered Tortilla Pie

This is a fun meal! Layering tortillas with beans, then baking and cutting into wedges, turns simple ingredients into something almost festive. While I usually make this with one type of bean, you could easily use two different types if you have leftover beans stashed in the freezer. Pintos and black beans go well together. This is excellent when served with a salad.

- 4 cups cooked beans, divided
- 1 cup salsa, divided
- ¼ teaspoon garlic powder
- ½ teaspoon ground cumin

- ¼ teaspoon dried oregano
- ½ teaspoon dried parsley (or use fresh)
- 2 tablespoons fresh cilantro, chopped (optional)
- 2 small tomatoes, chopped (or use ½ can diced tomatoes, well drained)
- 10 tortillas
- 2 cups shredded cheese (cheddar is great, or use your favorite)

Preheat oven to 400 degrees.

In a bowl, mash 2 cups of beans with a fork. Add ½ cup salsa, garlic powder, and cumin. Stir to mix.

In a separate bowl, add the remaining 2 cups of beans, ½ cup salsa, oregano, parsley, cilantro (if using), and tomatoes. Stir to mix.

Place 2 tortillas side by side on a cookie sheet or large baking dish. Spread a layer of the mashed beans on each tortilla, keeping it about ½ inch from the edge. I estimate around ⅓ cup for each tortilla. Top with a nice sprinkle of cheese.

Layer a second tortilla on each tortilla/bean/cheese. Top with about ½ cup of whole bean mixture and then add a nice sprinkle of cheese.

Put a third tortilla on each. Spread a layer of the mashed beans on each tortilla (around ⅓ cup on each), keeping it about ½ inch from the edge. Top with a nice sprinkle of cheese.

Add a fourth tortilla on each. Top with about ½ cup of whole bean mixture (you can use it all). Add a nice sprinkle of cheese.

Add a fifth tortilla on each. Spread the remaining mashed beans over the top. Cover the baking dish or cookie sheet by putting toothpicks in the tortilla pie and suspending foil over the top.

Bake until heated through, about 40 minutes. Remove from oven and uncover. Sprinkle with remaining shredded cheese. After the cheese melts, cut into wedges and serve. This is excellent topped with additional salsa, sour cream, jalapeños, cilantro, etc.

Meal Options 2

- Pinto Beans with Cornbread
- Taco Salad Platter
- Pinto Bean Chili

Beans with cornbread! This was my dad's favorite meal. He loved the cornbread topped with honey butter. Sometimes he'd crumble the cornbread in with his beans and eat it that way. Every time we have beans with a pan of cornbread, I'm taken back to these memories of my dad. One slight difference to my way of making this dish, compared to how my parents did, is the addition of browned onions. There's something about adding a few tablespoons of these richly flavored onions that really sets off the flavor of the pinto beans.

For Day 1, the pinto beans are the main dish. You'll need 3 cups of beans for Day 2, and 4 cups of beans (with the juice) for Day 3. I like to take out the amount I'll need for future days before serving the meal on Day 1. Any leftover beans can be frozen in 1-cup containers for later use or served for lunches during the week. I also make a double batch of rice so I have enough for both Day 1 and Day 2.

Day 1

Pinto Beans with Cornbread

Lightly browned onions are delicious with this! Slice two or three yellow onions and sauté them in a healthy fat. Sprinkle with a little salt and avoid stirring too much so they become a nicely browned color. They should be slightly brown and soft throughout, but still hold their shape. This takes about ten minutes.

When they are done, remove from the pan and add a half cup of broth (or water) to deglaze the pan. Scrape up any browned bits and let cook for about a minute to reduce the broth. Add the onions back into the pan and let cook another minute so the broth can mostly evaporate.

The beans should be seasoned simply with salt and pepper. Family members can then add additional seasonings at the table. The beans topped with the onions tastes amazing. You can add a side salad or other green vegetable to round out this meal.

Day 2

Taco Salad Platter

This is a delicious main dish salad! It's so easy and adaptable to your specific needs. The main components are beans (any variety), lettuce (your choice of style), chips (so many options!), ground or shredded meat (optional), additional veggies, and a yummy dressing (I'll share two of my favorites).

This salad begs for some crunch! So, the first thing to do is decide on your chip. You have options. The easiest is to purchase your favorite tortilla chip. There are some decent brands available without terrible ingredients, but they do tend to be pricey.

Making tortilla chips is a more economical option and you can better control your ingredients. My friend Wardee makes her tortilla chips out of sourdough. I've done this, and they are delicious but are also very hands on. Another option is to buy or make corn tortillas, heat them in the oven until brown and crispy, then use a knife or pizza cutter to cut the tortillas into chips.

Even with making the tortillas from scratch, this is a fairly simple process. No tortilla press? No problem—just roll them out. They don't need to be perfect for chips; just make sure to roll them thin enough.

If you'd like to add meat to this salad, you can use your favorite ground meat or leftover roast, chicken, turkey, or pork diced or shredded. This is a great way to use items stashed in the fridge or freezer. I've even done this with scrambled eggs and had excellent results. No meat? Don't fret! The beans are enough.

Method

If making your chips, do that first.

Brown the ground meat (if using) until cooked through. If using leftover meat, dice or shred it and then put in a pan to heat. Add the beans to the meat (both are optional) and warm through. For a meat-free taco salad, heat the beans thoroughly. If using eggs, scramble them separately.

While the beans are cooking, cut or shred the lettuce and place in a salad bowl. You can use one type of lettuce or a combination.

Take out a large cutting board and prepare any vegetables or toppers you'd like to use. We like tomatoes, sliced olives, minced onion (or green onion), avocado, green pepper, green chilies (the kind from a can or jar), and shredded cheese. I cut and serve directly from the cutting board. Add the chips to the board too!

When it's time to serve, everyone makes their own salad, adding whatever toppers they'd like. Then finish it off with dressing.

Sour Cream Salsa Dressing

Combine equal parts sour cream and salsa. If it's too thick, add a little milk as needed.

Thousand with a Kick

- 1 cup mayonnaise
- ¼ cup ketchup
- 2 tablespoon apple cider vinegar
- 1 cup salsa

- 2 tablespoon dry sweetener (such as Sucanat or Rapadura) or a dash of liquid stevia

Combine mayo (homemade mayonnaise is delicious in this recipe), ketchup, vinegar, salsa, and dry sweetener (if using stevia, hold off adding until the end) and mix well. Salt and pepper to taste. If using stevia, add now and mix again.

Day 3

Pinto Bean Chili

While I make chili often, I don't really have a recipe. I tend to create it while I'm standing at the stove. I use beans (with the broth they were cooked in), meat (if I have it), onions, chili powder, cumin (lots of cumin!), garlic powder, tomatoes, salt, and pepper. I fiddle with it until it tastes good.

For something a little more structured, use my Navajo Taco Chili recipe in Meal Options 3 as a guide. A pan of cornbread is always good with a bowl of chili.

Meal Options 3

- Pinto Beans and Tortillas
- Breakfast Burritos
- Navajo Tacos

Another memory of my dad, from pinto bean night, was him scooping up beans with a piece of tortilla. While cornbread was the preferred accompaniment for pinto beans, if things got too crazy and the cornbread wasn't made, we'd have tortillas. While my dad would use a spoon to add pinto beans to a small piece of tortilla, like a scoop, my younger brother would lay out his tortilla, putting a line of beans down the middle and top with ketchup, then roll it up to eat. Homemade or store-bought tortillas both work well for this. If making tortillas from scratch, be sure to make enough for your Day 2 dish.

For Day 1, the pinto beans are the main dish. You'll need 3 cups of beans for Day 2, and 4 cups of beans (with the juice) for Day 3. I like to take out the amount I'll need for future days before Day 1 is served. Any leftover beans can be frozen in 1-cup containers for later use or served for lunches during the week.

Day 1

Pinto Beans and Tortillas

Simply serve beans with flour tortillas and your choice of vegetable.

Day 2

Breakfast Burritos

Breakfast for dinner is always a treat.

And this one goes together super quick. Scramble some eggs. Cook some bacon or sausage if you'd like. Heat up the beans (maybe season it lightly with chili powder and cumin). Slice up an avocado. Shred some cheese. Wrap it all up in your favorite flour or corn tortilla. Finish it off with salsa and sour cream. Yum!

Day 3

Navajo Tacos

This is my husband's most requested pinto bean dish! The fry bread is the "taco shell." It's a wonderfully puffy little pastry that is placed on the plate (either whole or torn into pieces) and topped with a delicious chili-like sauce and then piled high with your favorite toppers such as lettuce, shredded cheese, tomatoes, salsa, sour cream, onions, etc. If you do not keep a sourdough starter, the fry bread can be made with your favorite bread dough.

The Chili

- ¼ to 1 pound of ground beef (optional)
- Coconut oil (if needed)
- 1 onion, diced
- 1 clove garlic, minced
- 4 cups cooked pinto beans with juice
- 1 can tomato paste
- ½ to 1 cup beef broth or water
- Sea salt, to taste
- Black pepper, to taste

In a cast iron skillet, cook the beef and half of the onion. Reserve the other half for a topper. Add a little coconut oil if needed for the onion to cook well.

When the ground beef is finished, add garlic, beans, tomato paste, and ½ cup of broth. Simmer for 30 minutes or so while you cook the fry bread, adding additional broth as needed. You'll want the chili to be on the saucy side. The fry bread will soak up the sauce and be amazingly delicious.

You can also use leftover chili. If it's not saucy enough, add additional broth or water.

The Sourdough Fry Bread

(Start early morning or the night before)

- ½ cup sourdough starter
- 1 cup milk
- 2 ½ cups whole wheat flour
- ¼ teaspoon sea salt
- Coconut oil

Mix all ingredients until combined. Cover with a cloth and let sit for 7 to 24 hours.

When ready to fry, stir in ¼ teaspoon of sea salt. The dough will be fairly sticky and should stir easily. Don't over work it, just get the salt blended in.

In a large skillet or pan (I use a deep cast iron skillet), heat about an inch of coconut oil. While it's heating up, shape your dough into patties, using flour as necessary to keep the dough from sticking to your hands.

When the oil is hot enough for a small piece of dough to sizzle, carefully put the patties in the oil to cook. When the bottom is brown (about 2 minutes), gently flip them over. Cook until the second side is brown and then put them on a cloth or paper towel to drain. Repeat with the remainder of the dough.

To Assemble

Put the fry bread on your plate. Add a ladle full (more or less) of the chili. Top with lettuce, onions, tomatoes, cheese, salsa, sour cream, or anything else that you enjoy on tacos.

This recipe is so delicious and is a simple meal to make.

Bonus Tip: Leftover fry bread can make a sweet treat when drizzled with or dipped in honey. They reheat very well in the oven as well as in a skillet or toaster. We've been known to have them for breakfast, topped with butter and cinnamon sugar or apple butter. Fry bread is extremely versatile and tastes amazing.

Bonus Recipe

Taco Soup

- ¼ to ½ pound ground beef or game (optional)
- 1 medium onion, chopped
- 1 tablespoon chili powder
- 2 teaspoons ground cumin
- ¼ to ½ teaspoon ground cayenne pepper
- 1 teaspoon paprika

- 2 cloves garlic, finely minced (or ¼ teaspoon garlic powder)
- Cooked pinto or red beans plus their juice
- 1 (14 ounce) can diced tomatoes, undrained
- 2 cups frozen corn or 1 can corn
- 1 (4 ounce) can green chilies, undrained
- Additional broth or water as needed
- Sea salt, to taste
- Black pepper, to taste

In a large soup pot, brown the ground beef (if using) and onions. Stir in the chili powder, cumin, cayenne pepper, and paprika. Allow to cook for a minute or two so the flavors can meld.

Add the garlic and stir, then add the beans, bean juice, tomatoes, corn, and green chilies. Stir well and heat through. Add salt and pepper to taste, plus additional broth or water as needed to make a soup-like consistency.

Top with shredded cheese, clabber cheese, sour cream, tortilla chips/tortilla strips, chopped onion or green onions, chopped tomato, or your favorite toppers.

For the tortilla chips/strips, I use leftover tortillas cut in either triangles or strips and lightly fried in coconut oil.

Note: This dish only uses ½ pound of ground meat, but you can certainly add more or even omit entirely if desired. I like to use the other half pound of beef as a pizza topping the next night, or I'll brown it and freeze for future use.

White Beans

I use the generic phrase of *white beans* for navy, small white, and Great Northern. Cannellini, Lima, and Baby Lima are also classified as white beans, but these are not beans I cook with, and I am not sure if they'll work in these suggestions. If you do try Cannellini or Lima beans, let me know how they turn out!

I've found small white beans to be the "plainest" of the white beans; they tend to take on other flavors well, without being overbearing on their own. They also cook the quickest. Great Northern beans have a slightly nutty texture and hold their shape quite well. Navy are also nutty, but they're very creamy and are my preference.

Feel free to omit the meat in these recipes if you don't want or have it. All these meals can be made meat-free; when combining beans with a whole grain, you'll end up with a complete protein.

Meal Options 1

- Fasooli
- Crispy Pan-Fried Beans and Wilted Greens
- Sauerkraut and Bean Soup

The Day 3 meal, Sauerkraut and Bean Soup, may not be quite what you expect. Many people are familiar with the limp sauerkraut found in a can—this is not the same. This recipe calls for raw, probiotic-rich kraut. You can purchase this in the refrigerator section of health-food stores, or you can make it yourself with very little time and effort for a huge cost savings. It's so easy! Traditional Cooking School teaches an easy no-pound method.

You'll need 3 cups of beans for Day 1, 4 cups for Day 2, and 3 cups for Day 3. Any leftover beans can be frozen in 1-cup containers for later use or served for lunches during the week. I also make a double batch of rice so I have enough for both Day 1 and Day 2.

Day 1

Fasooli

This is one of my favorites! It's inspired by my friend Wardee from Traditional Cooking School's favorite childhood dishes. I've made some slight changes to adapt for the Stretchy Beans concept.

- 1 onion, chopped
- 2 to 3 cloves garlic, minced (or ½ teaspoon garlic powder)
- 3 cups cooked white beans
- 1 can tomato paste
- 3 cups broth or water
- 2 teaspoons sea salt
- ½ teaspoon black pepper
- Cooked rice, brown or white

In a soup pot, sauté onions until translucent.

In a bowl, mix tomato paste with broth until smooth.

When the onions are soft, stir in the garlic and then immediately follow with the tomato paste mixture. Mix well, then add beans, salt, and pepper and warm through. Taste and add additional salt if needed. Serve over rice.

Day 2

Crispy Pan-Fried Beans and Wilted Greens

This dish was a happy find! The original recipe calls for za'atar, a Middle Eastern herb and spice blend. This isn't something I can buy locally, and I haven't gone the online ordering route. Instead, I substitute it with dried thyme, cumin, marjoram, and toasted sesame seeds. The end result is delicious! And it's extra delicious when served with a crusty bread.

- Swiss chard, kale, collard and/or spinach (about a pound)
- 2 onions, thinly sliced
- Healthy fat
- 4 cloves garlic, minced
- 4 cups cooked white beans
- Juice from 1 lemon (about 3 tablespoons)
- 1 teaspoon dried thyme, ground in a mortar and pestle
- 1 teaspoon ground cumin
- ¼ teaspoon marjoram (optional)
- 2 teaspoons sea salt
- 2 teaspoons toasted sesame seeds (optional)

Cut out the stems from the greens and then cut into bite-sized pieces. Slice the leaves into strips.

In a skillet, sauté the onion in about a tablespoon of fat until very soft (about 8 to 10 minutes). Add garlic and the chopped stems, stirring for a couple of minutes, then transfer to a bowl.

In your now-empty pan, heat up enough oil to cover the bottom of the pan, then add 1 cup of beans, spreading into a single layer. Let the beans cook for two minutes, without stirring. Then stir, spread into a single layer again, and cook for 2 additional minutes. Remove the beans from the skillet and place in a cooking dish in a warm oven. Repeat this step until all the beans are crispy and fried.

Add the chard leaves, thyme, cumin, marjoram, toasted sesame seeds (or the za'atar if using), and another teaspoon of salt into the beans, stirring for about 3 to 5 minutes until the chard is wilted and tender.

Stir in the onion mixture, lemon zest, and lemon juice, adding more juice or seasonings to taste if needed.

Dish out the servings and drizzle a little olive oil over each dish. Serve with rice.

Day 3

Sauerkraut and Bean Soup

Raw, probiotic-rich sauerkraut is the secret to this gut-friendly dish. You can buy fresh sauerkraut or, for a fraction of the cost, make your own. This soup is delicious with rolls or slices of well-buttered bread.

- 2 quarts broth, bean broth, water, or a combination
- 3 cups cooked white beans
- ¼ teaspoon garlic powder
- ¼ to 1 pound ground meat (optional; beef, wild game, chicken, turkey, pork, or sausage)
- Sea salt, to taste
- Black pepper, to taste
- 2 cups fresh sauerkraut

Put the beans and broth in a large pot and bring to a boil on high heat, skimming if necessary. Reduce heat to simmer. Add garlic and uncooked ground meat (if using).

Simmer 15 minutes, covered, or until meat is thoroughly cooked. Salt and pepper to taste.

Remove from heat and uncover. Let it cool until it's 115 degrees, then stir in the sauerkraut. The cooling stage is important. Because the sauerkraut is raw, you want to keep it raw. If you heat it above 115 degrees, you will lose nutritional value.

Meal Options 2

- White Beans and Rice
- White Beans and Cabbage
- White Bean Soup

You'll need 4 cups of beans for Day 1, 2 cups for Day 2, and 4 cups for Day 3. Any leftover beans can be frozen in 1-cup containers for later use or served for lunches during the week.

Day 1

White Beans and Rice

A delicious combination of sautéed vegetables and (optional) meat really makes the humble white bean stand out.

- 1 pound smoked sausage, sliced and cut into quarters (or bulk ground sausage) (optional)
- ½ pound bacon (optional)
- 1 tablespoon healthy fat
- 1 medium onion, diced
- ½ bell pepper (any color), diced
- 1 stalk celery, diced
- 2 or 3 carrots, peeled and diced
- ½ teaspoon garlic powder
- 1 can petite diced tomatoes (if you like a spicier dish, use the kind with peppers)
- 1 tablespoon dried parsley, crushed
- 4 cups cooked white beans, with some bean broth remaining
- Sea salt, to taste
- Black pepper, to taste
- Hot cooked rice

If using sausage, cook it in a large soup pot or saucepan until browned. Remove and drain grease. In the same pan, add the bacon (if using) and cook until crisp. Remove the bacon and drain on paper towels.

In the same pan, cook the onion, pepper, celery, and carrots in your choice of healthy fat.

When the veggies are soft, add garlic powder, tomatoes, parsley, and beans with bean broth. If you're using sausage and/or bacon, add the cooked meats now. Stir until mixed, then simmer about 5 minutes to slightly thicken. Salt and pepper to taste.

Serve over rice. This is delicious with hot sauce added at the table.

Day 2

White Beans and Cabbage

The combination of potatoes, beans, and cabbage make this a hearty stir-fry-style dish. This recipe is adapted from Steamy Kitchen's White Beans and Cabbage.

- 2 tablespoons healthy fat
- 2 medium potatoes, finely diced
- ½ teaspoon dried thyme
- ½ onion, minced
- 2 cups cooked white beans
- 3 cups green cabbage, finely shredded
- ½ teaspoon sea salt
- ¼ teaspoon black pepper

In a large skillet, heat healthy fat over medium-high heat. Add the diced potatoes. Cook for 5 to 7 minutes, stirring frequently, until the potatoes begin to soften.

Stir in the thyme, onion, and beans. Spread everything out and let cook for 2 minutes without stirring. Stir and let cook an additional 2 minutes. Repeat until the beans are browned and the onions and potatoes are soft and slightly golden.

Add the cabbage, then stir and cook for 1 minute. Add salt and pepper. Stir and cook until the cabbage is wilted. Add additional salt and pepper to taste.

Day 3

White Bean Soup

Quick, easy, creamy, and delicious. The bacon is optional but highly recommended.

- 1 medium onion, finely diced
- 2 tablespoons healthy fat
- 5 cups chicken or vegetable broth, bean broth, water, or a combination
- 4 cups cooked beans
- 2 bay leaves
- ¾ teaspoon dried thyme
- ¾ cup carrots, peeled and diced
- 5 to 6 strips cooked bacon (optional)
- ¾ cup milk
- Sea salt, to taste

In a large pot, sauté onions in healthy fat. Add broth, beans, carrots, bay leaves, thyme, and bacon. Bring to a low boil over medium-low heat for 25 to 30 minutes.

Remove bay leaves and stir in milk.

Blend half of the soup until it's creamy. To do this, either remove half of the soup and use an immersion blender on the half still left in the pot, or put the removed half in a blender. Whichever way works for you, just make sure the blended half is nice and creamy. Then reunite the blended soup with the unblended soup. Stir together and salt to taste.

Bonus Recipes

BBQ Style Beans

Several years ago, one of my girls asked for baked beans. Instead of making an oven version, I made them on the stovetop using the barbeque sauce for my Short Rib recipe as a base.

- 1 cup ketchup (HFCS free) or tomato sauce
- ¼ cup tamari or naturally fermented soy sauce
- 2 tablespoons olive oil
- 2 tablespoons honey (or ¼ cup Sucanat or another natural sweetener)
- 2 tablespoons molasses (optional)
- ½ teaspoon sea salt
- ¼ teaspoon black pepper
- 1 teaspoon garlic powder (or 3 cloves fresh garlic, minced)
- 1 cup water or broth
- ¼ cup dried onion (or ½ cup fresh onion, minced)
- 4 cups cooked beans
- ½ to 2 cups precooked meat (optional)

Combine tomato sauce, soy sauce, olive oil, sweetener, molasses, salt, pepper, garlic, broth, and onion in a stew pot. Mix well and bring to a boil.

Turn down heat and allow to simmer for 5 to 10 minutes to blend the flavors and soften the onion. Add beans and meat (if using) and heat through.

This tastes excellent served over rice or with a slice of cornbread.

Bean Stew

Inspired by Great Northern Bean Stew from Traditional Cooking School. This is especially hearty when served over brown rice. The optional nutritional yeast adds a "cheesy" flavor and nice consistency. In place of the nutritional yeast, you could shred cheese over individual bowls at serving.

- ½ to 2 pounds ground meat (optional; beef, wild game, lamb, chicken, etc.)
- 2 small onions, diced
- 2 cups broth or water (may need additional depending on quantity of bean broth)
- 1 (6 ounce) can tomato paste
- 4 cups cooked white beans, with bean broth
- 2 teaspoons sea salt, plus additional to taste
- ½ teaspoon black pepper
- 1 tablespoon dried basil
- 1 teaspoon dried thyme
- 1 teaspoon dried oregano
- ¼ cup nutritional yeast (optional, but recommended.)

In a large soup pot, brown the meat (if using) and onions. Turn to medium heat when finished.

In a bowl, whisk tomato paste and broth until smooth. Add tomato paste mixture and all ingredients except nutritional yeast to pot. Bring to a boil.

Reduce heat, then cover and simmer for 15 minutes. Stir in nutritional yeast, if using. Add additional broth or water if the soup is too thick.

Creamy White Chili

Adapted from a Taste of Home recipe, this creamy chili is quick, easy, and delicious.

- 1 medium onion, chopped
- 1 tablespoon healthy fat
- 1 ½ teaspoons garlic powder
- 4 cups white beans, cooked
- 4 cups broth, water, bean broth, or a combination
- 1 (4 ounce) can chopped green chiles, undrained
- 1 teaspoon sea salt
- 1 teaspoon ground cumin
- 1 teaspoon dried oregano
- ½ teaspoon black pepper
- ¼ teaspoon cayenne pepper (optional)
- ½ to 2 cups cooked chicken, shredded or diced (optional)
- 1 cup sour cream
- ½ cup heavy whipping cream (optional)
- Tortilla chips (optional)

- Cheddar cheese, shredded (optional)
- 1 jalapeno pepper, seeded and sliced (optional)

In a large saucepan, sauté the onion in fat until translucent. Stir in the garlic powder, beans, broth, green chiles, and seasonings. Bring to a boil. Reduce heat and simmer uncovered for 30 minutes. If using chicken, add it during the last five minutes of simmering time.

Remove from the heat and then stir in sour cream and heavy cream (if using). If desired, top with tortilla chips, cheese, and jalapeños.

Black Beans

When I was in my early twenties, I dabbled with being a vegetarian. An experienced vegetarian friend introduced me to black beans. The dabbling only lasted a few weeks, but black beans have remained a part of my diet since then.

Usually, on night one of black beans, I'll make an easy black bean and rice dish—and I almost always make a double batch of rice to turn into Stretchy Rice for either supper or breakfast the next day. We love Butterscotch Rice and also Rice Pancakes.

On night two, we'll have a burrito or tostada-style meal.

Night three is often a soup, chili, or skillet dish. I find these types of meals work great for using up the remaining beans.

And remember, you can skip the meat in any of these recipes since beans and grains make a complete protein. Use these suggestions as a guide to make Stretchy Black Beans work for you.

Meal Options 1

- Black Beans and Rice Platter
- Stuffed Burritos
- Coconut Curried Black Bean Soup

For Day 1, the black beans are the main dish. For Day 2, you'll need 2 to 3 cups of beans (if you are using meat or eggs in this dish, you use less beans). For Day 3, you'll need 4 cups of beans.

I like to take out the amount I'll need for future days before serving on Day 1. Any leftover beans can be frozen in 1-cup containers for later use or served for lunches during the week. I also make a double batch of rice so I have enough for both Day 1 and Day 2.

Day 1

Black Beans and Rice Platter

Around the same time my friend introduced me to black beans, I lived within walking distance of a Macheezmo Mouse restaurant. This was a small Portland, Oregon, based chain that touted healthy Mexican food at a great price. Every so often, I would load up my two young girls in the double stroller and we'd walk to The Mouse. The three of us would share a Vegetarian Platter: a plate loaded with black beans, brown rice, salad greens, broccoli, salsa, guacamole, and a couple of tortillas. Topped with their famous Boss Sauce, it was amazing. And so much food! Sadly, Macheezmo Mouse closed after the death of the founder. In recent years, I've tried to find a recipe online for the Boss Sauce, but I haven't found one with the same flavors—slightly hot, slightly sweet, with a hint of orange. It was *soooo* good.

For my Black Beans and Rice Platter, we use Cholula or a similar hot sauce and top the greens with a yummy vinaigrette, a slight variation on Whole New Mom's 5-Ingredient Dressing. The dressing can go over the top of the beans and rice too. Feel free to add steamed broccoli and serve with a couple of tortillas. It's not the same as the Macheezmo Mouse Vegetarian Platter, but it's still delicious.

5-Ingredient Dressing

- ¼ cup olive oil (mild)
- ¼ cup avocado oil (can use ½ cup olive oil if you don't have avocado oil)
- ½ cup rice wine vinegar or apple cider vinegar
- ¼ teaspoon garlic powder (or use a clove of finely minced fresh garlic)
- 1 teaspoon sea salt
- ¼ cup nutritional yeast

Put oil and vinegar in a pint-size mason jar. Whisk well to combine. Add additional ingredients and whisk again. Stir before serving. Add extra nutritional yeast if you'd like a thicker dressing.

Day 2

Stuffed Burritos

These burritos are super easy and versatile, and they can be made with any ingredients you have on hand.

- Cooked meat (optional; shredded or ground beef, chicken, turkey, venison, etc.) *
- 1 ½ cups broth, water, or a combination
- 1 to 3 tablespoons chili powder
- 1 tablespoon ground cumin
- ¼ teaspoon garlic powder
- Sea salt, to taste
- Black pepper, to taste
- Dash of cayenne pepper

- 2 to 3 cups cooked beans
- Cooked rice
- Shredded cheese
- Tortillas
- Toppers, such as lettuce, cabbage, sauerkraut, sour cream, salsa, avocado, etc.

Season the meat (if using). If you're using a roast or chicken, cube or shred the meat and add about 1 ½ cups of broth or water while heating gently. Add chili powder, cumin, and garlic powder; salt and pepper to taste; and a dash of cayenne pepper. You can also add a small can of tomato sauce for additional flavor.

Warm up your precooked beans. You can leave them whole, lightly mash them with a potato masher, or puree them in the food processor. Whatever sounds good to you and works with the kind of day you're having.

Season the rice with salt, pepper, and garlic powder (if desired), then assemble your burritos.

*Another protein option is scrambled eggs, making a yummy breakfast burrito. Allow at least one egg per person.

Day 3

Curried Coconut Black Bean Soup

This is a savory, creamy, and quick-cooking recipe adapted from Veganosity. This soup is delicious with a side salad and dinner rolls/bread.

- 4 cups cooked black beans
- 4 cups broth or water
- 1 medium onion, diced
- 3 cloves garlic, minced (or ½ teaspoon garlic powder)
- 1 (16 ounce) can coconut milk (light will reduce fat and calories; regular will make it creamier)
- 1 ½ teaspoons ground curry
- 1 ½ teaspoons ground cumin
- ½ teaspoon sea salt
- Juice of a small lime (about 2 tablespoons)
- Black pepper, to taste

Blend all ingredients, except lime juice and black pepper, in a food processor or blender until smooth and creamy. Pour the mixture into a saucepan and heat to boiling. Alternately, combine ingredients (minus lime juice and black pepper) in a saucepan and use your immersion blender to process until smooth.

Reduce heat and simmer for 20 to 25 minutes. Add lime juice and a sprinkle of black pepper. Taste for seasoning, adding additional salt and pepper as desired.

Meal Options 2

- Black Bean Rice Bowls
- Black Bean and Cheese Quesadillas
- Creamy Black Bean Chili

The star in this rotation is delicious burritos bowls! These burritos bowls are completely customizable, allowing each person to add their preferred ingredients.

You'll need 4 cups of beans for Day 1, 2 cups for Day 2, and 4 cups for Day 3. Any leftover beans can be frozen in 1-cup containers for later use or served for lunches during the week.

Day 1

Black Bean Rice Bowls

Adapted from Black Bean Rice Bowls by Traditional Cooking School.

- 4 cups cooked black beans
- 1 cup broth (can also use juice from the cooked beans or water)
- 1 teaspoons sea salt
- ½ teaspoon black pepper
- 1 tablespoon ground cumin
- 1 tablespoon paprika
- 2 tablespoons nutritional yeast (optional but recommended)
- Seasoned shredded chicken or other meat (optional)
- Cooked corn (optional)
- Cooked rice

Combine 2 cups of beans plus remaining ingredients in a saucepan over low heat.

Mash with a potato masher until smooth. Add the remaining 2 cups of beans and mash a little more. I like to keep this on the chunky side.

To serve, put rice in the bottom of each person's bowl. Top with a scoop or two of seasoned black beans, meat and corn (if using), plus choice of toppers, such as Chipotle Sauce (recipe below), diced onions, sliced olives, diced avocado, shredded cheese, cilantro, sour cream, salsa, etc.

Chipotle Sauce

A single chipotle chili in adobo sauce is the basis for this delicious sauce. Chipotle chiles are dried, smoked jalapeños. Adobo is a tangy, slightly sweet red sauce. Put them together in a can and they become a versatile pantry staple. The cans are only 7 ounces for many of the brands available. Since you are only using 1 chili and the sauce attached to that chili, the remainder of the can should be stashed in the freezer for future use.

- 1 cup sour cream
- 1 single chipotle chili with the clinging sauce
- ¼ teaspoon garlic powder
- 1 tablespoon lime juice
- ¼ teaspoon salt (or more to taste)

Combine all ingredients in a blender or food processor (or in a bowl, using an immersion blender). Blend until smooth and creamy. A little of this sauce goes a long way. You want a consistency suitable for drizzling. Add a little milk or water as needed to thin it out.

Day 2

Black Bean and Cheese Quesadillas

These quesadillas are so quick and easy to make.

- 2 cups cooked black beans (with little to no bean juice)
- Shredded cheese
- Tortillas

Mash or puree the beans and then spread a generous bean layer on the tortillas. Sprinkle with shredded cheese (to your own taste) and top with a second tortilla.

In a hot cast iron skillet, grill until the first side is lightly brown (I like to add a little butter so the tortilla crisps nicely). Carefully flip and repeat on the second side.

If desired, you can add thinly shredded meat to the pureed beans and cheese before grilling.

Day 3

Creamy Black Bean Chili

Adapted from Classic Chili Recipe by Traditional Cooking School. This is delicious with cornbread.

- 1 onion, diced
- 3 cloves garlic, diced
- 1 bell pepper (any color), diced

- ½ pound ground meat (optional)
- 2 to 3 tablespoons sea salt
- ½ teaspoon ground pepper
- 1 ½ to 2 tablespoons ground cumin
- 1 tablespoon paprika
- 1 teaspoon dried oregano
- 1 teaspoon dried thyme
- 4 cups cooked black beans
- 1 can tomato paste
- 4 cups water or broth

In a large soup pot, sauté the onion, bell peppers, and garlic until soft. If using meat, brown alongside the veggies. When the veggies are soft and the meat is browned, add the spices. Then add the beans to the pan.

In a bowl, mix tomato paste and water until smooth, then stir it into the veggie and bean mixture. Simmer for 20 to 30 minutes. Taste for seasoning.

Top with sour cream, onion, cheese, avocado, etc. as desired.

Meal Options 3

- Easy Black Bean and Yellow Rice
- Black Bean Tostadas
- Creamy Black Bean Soup

Are you tired of boring white rice? Jazz it up! The addition of turmeric changes the color and gives a slight variation to the flavor.

You'll need 4 cups of beans for Day 1, 2 to 3 cups for Day 2 (if you are using meat or eggs in this dish, you use less beans), and 4 cups of beans plus the juice they were cooked in for Day 3. Any leftover beans can be frozen in 1-cup containers for later use or served for lunches during the week.

Day 1

Easy Black Beans and Yellow Rice

Yellow rice? Yep! The addition of turmeric and garlic really sets off this flavorful rice base. Adapted from The Spruce Eats Easy Black Bean and Yellow Rice.

- 1 cup white rice, uncooked
- ½ cup onion, chopped
- ¼ cup celery, chopped
- ¼ cup green pepper, chopped
- 4 cups cooked black beans
- 1 (14.5 ounces) can diced tomatoes, undrained
- 1 teaspoon Sucanat or sugar
- 1 teaspoon dried oregano
- ½ teaspoon dried basil
- 1 teaspoon garlic powder, divided
- ¼ teaspoon black pepper
- ½ teaspoon sea salt
- ¼ to ½ teaspoon hot sauce
- ½ teaspoon ground turmeric

Cook rice according to package instructions.

Sauté onion, celery, and green pepper until tender. Stir in beans, tomatoes, Sucanat, oregano, basil, ½ teaspoon garlic powder, pepper, sea salt, and hot sauce. Mix well and then simmer for 5 minutes.

To the cooked rice, stir in turmeric and ½ teaspoon garlic powder. Salt rice to taste.

Serve black beans over yellow rice.

Day 2

Black Bean Tostadas

Whenever we go visit the Northern California town where my husband grew up, we always have lunch at a fast-food Mexican place. It's delicious and very inexpensive. I always order the Tostada Salad. These Black Bean Tostadas were inspired by the restaurant dish.

- Cooked meat (optional; shredded or ground beef, chicken, turkey, venison, etc.)
- 2 to 3 cups cooked beans
- Cooked rice
- Shredded cheese
- Lettuce or cabbage, shredded (or use a combination of lettuce and cabbage)
- Toppers, such as sauerkraut, sour cream, salsa, avocado, etc., or homemade Ranch Dressing to make it more of a salad (recipe below)
- Crispy tortillas

If using meat, season the meat and prepare. If you are using a roast or chicken, cube or shred the meat and add about 1 ½ cups of broth or water while heating gently. Season with a little chili powder, cumin, and garlic powder; salt and pepper to taste; and a dash of cayenne pepper. I usually add a small can of tomato sauce also. Scrambled eggs can be used instead of shredded or cubed meat!

Warm up your precooked beans. You can leave them whole, lightly mash them with a potato masher, or puree them in the food processor. Whatever sounds good to you and works with the kind of day you are having.

Season the rice with salt, pepper, and garlic powder.

Cook flour or corn tortillas in butter to make them crispy. (Check out the Stretchy Pinto Bean or Resources sections for links to tortilla recipes.)

Lay out the tortilla, top with seasoned rice, beans, meat (or eggs, if using), and lettuce or cabbage. Pile it high! It should resemble a salad. Finish with additional toppers—the Ranch Dressing is especially good.

Ranch Dressing

Several years ago, we started making our own salad dressings. This not only helps our budget, but we know exactly what the ingredients are. Most of the time, my husband or I will simply combine ingredients and make a dressing of the day. But for tostadas, this Ranch Dressing recipe is perfect.

- 1 cup mayonnaise (homemade is best)

- 1 cup sour cream
- 1 tablespoon lemon juice
- 1 teaspoon dried parsley
- 1 teaspoon dried dill
- ½ teaspoon garlic powder
- 1 teaspoon dried chives (optional)
- Sea salt, to taste
- Black pepper, to taste

Combine all ingredients in a bowl and whisk until smooth. If it's too thick, this can be thinned with a little milk, cream, or cultured buttermilk. Store leftovers in the refrigerator, covered, for up to one week.

Day 3

Creamy Black Bean Soup

This is a family favorite. It's a great way to use up the last of a pot of beans and the juice they were cooked in. This recipe is based off Black Bean Soup in *Nourishing Traditions* by Sally Fallon.

- 1 medium onion, diced (or ¼ cup dehydrated onions)
- 2 tablespoons healthy fat
- 4 cups cooked beans and bean juice
- 2 cups broth (any kind) plus additional if needed (or use water)
- ½ cup red wine or kombucha (or use more broth)
- 2 cloves of garlic, minced
- 1 teaspoon ground cumin
- ¼ teaspoon red pepper flakes

- ¼ cup red wine vinegar
- Sea salt, to taste
- Black pepper, to taste

If using dehydrated onion, rehydrate in hot water until plump. Sauté onion (fresh or rehydrated) in oil until tender. Fresh onion will take 5 to 10 minutes; rehydrated onion only takes 1 to 2 minutes.

Add beans with bean juice, broth, and red wine. Bring to a boil and skim if needed. Add cumin, oregano, garlic, and red pepper flakes and then simmer for 15 minutes.

Depending on how much bean juice was originally added, you may need additional broth to keep it a soup consistency.

After simmering, puree with a handheld or immersion blender or very carefully puree in a standard blender in multiple batches.

Reheat and add red wine vinegar plus additional broth if it's too thick. We like this to be on the thick side, but you can adjust to the consistency you desire.

Serve topped with any or all of the following toppers: sour cream, salsa, shredded cheese, cilantro, or green onions.

Kidney Beans

Larger than pinto or black beans, with more of a sweet, meaty flavor, the thick-skinned kidney bean almost pops when you bite into it. They are also somewhat neutral, picking up the spices used in cooking. This gives a great opportunity for multiple flavors with your Stretchy Kidney Beans.

Kidney beans are treated differently than other types of beans because of the naturally occurring toxin that needs to be cooked out of them. Because of this, I add an extra step when cooking kidney beans.

After soaking them overnight and giving them a good rinse, I boil on the stovetop in fresh water for 10 minutes before finishing the cooking in the crockpot, Instant Pot, or an alternative cooking method. Also, I don't sprout kidney beans.

You may choose to do something different based on your research; this is just my preference for kidney beans.

Meal Options 1

- Jamaican-Style Beans and Rice
- Enchilada Casserole
- Cowboy Soup

If the only time you've ever experienced a kidney bean is from a can, you owe it to yourself to cook them fresh from dried beans! The taste is completely different. I was originally hesitant to add these to our Stretchy Beans options due to my experience with only canned kidney beans. Sure, the cans are fine—for what they are—but I couldn't imagine an entire meal of those mushy, tinny flavored beans. Cooking them from scratch eliminates the canned flavor and really focuses on the meaty, full flavor.

You'll need 4 cups of beans for Day 1, 3 cups for Day 2, and 3 cups for Day 3. Any leftover beans can be frozen in 1-cup containers for later use or served for lunches during the week.

Day 1

Jamaican-Style Beans and Rice

This is a modification of a recipe from *Nourishing Traditions* by Sally Fallon. Coconut milk makes this a wonderfully creamy dish. At around $2 a can, coconut milk can seem an extravagance when counting your pennies. I think the nutritional component of coconut milk, along with its deliciousness, makes it worth the slight splurge.

Coconut milk is considered a healthy fat and is rich in short and medium chain triglycerides. Healthy fats help prolong the feeling of satiety, helping you to feel full longer. This dish has a slight spice to it from the jalapeños. For my family, I stick with only one pepper—feel free to increase this amount if you like it hot!

- 4 cups cooked red kidney beans
- 6 to 8 cups broth (mild, such as chicken or vegetable), water, or a combination
- 1 can coconut milk (or 7 ounces creamed coconut)
- 1 bunch green onions, chopped

- 1 to 3 jalapeno peppers, seeded and chopped
- ½ teaspoon garlic powder (or 3 cloves fresh garlic, mashed)
- 2 teaspoons dried thyme
- 2 teaspoons sea salt
- ½ teaspoon black pepper
- 1 cup brown rice, soaked at least 7 hours and then drained

Combine ingredients in a large soup pot. If using creamed coconut, stir until it is melted. Start with 6 cups of broth or water, adding more if needed to cover the rice and beans by ½ to 1 inch. Bring to a boil, then cover and cook on the lowest heat for about 30 minutes or until the rice is soft.

Alternate directions: Cook the 1 cup of rice separately (this can be done in advance). Combine all ingredients, except the cooked rice, and simmer for 10 minutes until heated through. Stir in the cooked rice and heat for a few additional minutes.

Day 2

Enchilada Casserole

The addition of broth to the enchilada sauce adds an extra heartiness and a dash of nutrition. This casserole goes together very easily.

For the filling:

- ½ pound hamburger (optional)
- 3 cups cooked kidney beans

- ½ teaspoon chili powder
- 1 teaspoon ground cumin
- ¾ teaspoon sea salt
- ¼ teaspoon black pepper
- A few dashes cayenne pepper

For the enchilada sauce:

- 2 cups chicken broth
- 4 teaspoons chili powder
- 1 teaspoon ground cumin
- 2 teaspoons garlic powder
- ¾ teaspoon sea salt
- Pinch of ground cinnamon
- ¼ to ½ teaspoon sugar
- 3 tablespoons plus ¼ teaspoon flour
- 3 tablespoons coconut oil

Other:

- Tortillas (corn, sourdough, or flour)
- 3+ cups shredded cheddar cheese
- Toppers, such as sour cream, sliced olives, green onions, etc.

Filling

Brown the hamburger (if using), then add kidney beans and seasonings. Heat until warm throughout.

Enchilada Sauce

In a medium saucepan, heat coconut oil over medium-high heat. When hot, reduce to low heat and whisk in flour, stirring consistently for 1 to 2 minutes. Add chili powder and mix well.

Slowly add chicken broth and then turn to medium heat, mixing well. Stir in seasonings and bring to a boil, stirring constantly for 3 to 5 minutes. Remove from heat.

Assemble

Preheat oven to 350 degrees. Cover the bottom of a 9 x 13 pan with about ⅓ cup of enchilada sauce. Put down a layer of tortillas, half of the bean mixture, and 1 cup of cheese. Repeat with another layer of tortillas, the remaining bean mixture, and another cup of cheese. Finish it off with a final layer of tortillas and cheese.

Cover and bake for 30 minutes, then cook for an additional 10 minutes uncovered.

Top with sour cream, Latin American Sauerkraut (Cordito), sliced olives, green onions, etc.

Day 3

Cowboy Soup

This is a Tex-Mex style soup that goes together quickly and is the perfect way to use up leftover vegetables and rice. Add a dollop of sour cream on top and a slice of cornbread on the side.

- ½ pound ground meat (optional)
- 3 cups cooked kidney beans
- ½ to 1 onion, diced
- 1 can petite diced tomatoes (can use the kind with chilies added, if you prefer)
- 6 cups broth, water, or a combination
- 1 small can tomato sauce
- ½ teaspoon garlic powder
- 1 ½ cups frozen corn (or 1 can corn)
- Leftover vegetables (such as green beans, carrots, peas, or frozen mixed vegetables)
- Sea salt, to taste
- Black pepper, to taste
- 1 cup cooked rice (optional; adds heartiness, especially if skipping the meat)

Brown the hamburger (if using) and onions, then add the rest of the ingredients and heat through. Taste and adjust seasonings if needed.

Meal Options 2

- Rajma
- Southwestern Haystacks
- Sweet Potato Chili

There's so much variety in this rotation! And all of it screams comfort food.

You'll need 4 cups of beans for Day 1, 3 cups of beans for Day 2, and 3 cups for Day 3. Any leftover beans can be frozen in 1-cup containers for later use or served for lunches during the week.

Day 1

Rajma

I'm not going to lie; this is one of my favorite dishes. Rajma is red beans—Indian style. Beware, it does have a bit of spice to it. If you prefer a less spicy dish, use only one hot pepper and/or eliminate the red pepper flakes. Top with a dollop of yogurt (to cool it down) and serve over rice with sourdough flatbread or naan on the side.

- 2 tablespoons healthy fat (I love ghee in this dish, but any healthy fat will work)
- 1 small onion, diced
- 2 small hot chili peppers, diced (jalapeno or your favorite)
- ¾ teaspoon garlic powder (or 5 cloves fresh garlic, minced)
- 1 inch ginger, minced (or 2 teaspoons ground ginger)
- 1 teaspoon turmeric
- 1 teaspoon sea salt, plus additional to taste
- 5 tomatoes, chopped (or 1 can diced tomatoes)
- 1 teaspoon chili powder
- 1 small pinch dried red pepper flakes
- ¼ teaspoon cinnamon
- ¼ teaspoon black pepper
- ¼ teaspoon ground cumin
- 3 cups cooked kidney beans

Cook onion in fat over low heat until soft. Add peppers, garlic, and ginger. Stir to mix.

Add tomatoes, cooking until they break down and everything is hot. Stir in turmeric, salt, chili powder, red pepper flakes, cinnamon, black pepper, and cumin. Mix well. Add kidney beans and bring to a boil.

Reduce heat to a simmer and allow it to cook down until it's a gravy-like consistency (about 5 minutes).

Day 2

Southwestern Haystacks

This is another super easy comforting dish. We don't eat a lot of pasta, preferring less refined foods, but this one is worth the splurge. While I like elbow macaroni for this dish, you can use any shape you prefer. You can also replace the pasta with mashed potatoes or spaghetti squash.

- ½ pound hamburger (optional)
- 2 cups cooked kidney beans
- A couple of tomatoes, diced (or ½ can petite diced tomatoes)
- 1 cup corn (frozen or canned)
- ½ teaspoon garlic powder
- Sea salt, to taste
- Black pepper, to taste
- Cooked pasta (enough for your size family)
- Optional toppers, such as sour cream or shredded cheese

Cook pasta according to package directions.

In a large saucepan, cook hamburger (if using). When it is browned, add beans, tomatoes, corn, and garlic. Heat through. Salt and pepper to taste.

Serve over the pasta and then top with sour cream and shredded cheese.

Day 3

Sweet Potato Chili

In October, we often have a neighborhood chili feed. A couple of us cook up a few different types of chili dishes, and everyone else brings a side or dessert. At our last chili feed, I made this Sweet Potato Chili. It was a huge hit. Modified from Vegetarian Sweet Potato Chili from Cookie and Kate.

- 1 tablespoon healthy fat
- 1 medium onion, chopped
- 1 green bell pepper, chopped
- 1 red bell pepper, chopped (or use 2 green peppers)
- 1 medium sweet potato, peeled and cut into ½ inch cubes
- ½ teaspoon garlic powder (or 4 cloves fresh garlic, pressed)
- 1 tablespoon chili powder
- 1 teaspoon ground cumin
- ¼ teaspoon cayenne pepper (more if you like it spicy)
- 2 teaspoons unsweetened cocoa powder
- ¼ teaspoon ground cinnamon
- ½ teaspoon sea salt
- ¼ teaspoon black pepper
- 2 small (14.5 ounce) cans or 1 large (28 ounce) can diced tomatoes, undrained
- 3 cups cooked kidney beans

- 2 cups broth, water, or a combination
- Toppers such as sour cream, grated cheese, thinly sliced green onions and/or chopped cilantro

In a stockpot over medium heat, warm the fat until shimmering. Add the veggies and sprinkle with salt and pepper. Cook and stir until the onions are translucent, about 3 to 5 minutes.

Reduce the heat to low. Add all of the spices, giving it a stir to incorporate with the vegetables. Increase heat to medium, then stir in the tomatoes, beans, and broth. Bring the mixture to a gentle simmer.

Maintain the gentle simmer for about 45 minutes to 1 hour until the sweet potatoes are soft, stirring occasionally. Add additional salt and pepper to taste.

Garbanzo Beans (Chickpeas)

Garbanzo beans were not something I grew up eating, other than occasionally on a salad, "fresh" out of a can.

When I started cooking with them a few years ago, we discovered they were a quite tasty little bean—and quite different when prepared from the dry state compared to opening a can. They are incredibly versatile, and the size of them makes them almost "meaty." It's a welcome sensation when meat is limited in the diet!

Have you heard of aquafaba? This is the liquid leftover after cooking garbanzo and white beans. It's achieved popularity in the last several years as a substitute for egg whites. You can even whip it into a meringue! What a great, amazing money saver.

Tip: You should only use aquafaba from beans that were previously soaked, with the soaking water discarded. Also, if you're planning to use aquafaba as an egg white substitute, use only plain water for cooking as opposed to broth or a broth/water combination.

Meal Options 1

- Garbanzo Bean Curry
- Spinach with Garbanzo Beans
- Chickpea Tacos

Garbanzo beans or chickpeas? Is there a difference? Both names are used interchangeably to refer to the round, beige legume known as Kabuli Chickpeas. And that's what we're talking about, whether referring to Garbanzo Bean Curry or Chickpea Tacos. Chickpea is often the English name for the bean while Garbanzo is the Spanish name. There are also Desi Chickpeas which are smaller and variously colored. I don't think I've ever seen Desi Chickpeas in my stores or my online ordering options. If they are an option for you, you could certainly try them in these dishes and see if they work.

You'll need 4 cups of beans for Day 1, 3 cups for Day 2, and 2 cups for Day 3. Any leftover beans can be frozen in 1-cup containers for later use or served for lunches during the week. I also make a double batch of rice so I have enough for both Day 1 and Day 3.

Day 1

Garbanzo Bean Curry

The basis for this curry was a recipe found on the *Lentils and Rice* blog, my inspiration for my Stretchy Beans repertoire. The original recipe did not have the coconut milk. It was still delicious, just not as rich. Feel free to omit the coconut milk if you don't have room for it in your budget. Be sure to make sourdough flatbread or naan to go along with this. So good!

- ½ onion, minced
- 1 tablespoon coconut oil
- 1 to 3 tablespoons curry powder (or make your own)
- 1 teaspoon ground cumin
- 1 clove garlic, minced
- 3 tablespoons tomato paste

- 1 bag frozen green beans or okra
- 4 cups cooked garbanzo beans
- 2 cups of the broth the beans cooked in (or use water)
- 1 can diced tomatoes, undrained (or 3 fresh tomatoes, diced)
- 1 teaspoon sea salt
- ¼ teaspoon black pepper
- 1 can coconut milk

Over low heat, cook the onion in the coconut oil until soft, about 7 to 10 minutes.

Add the curry powder and cumin and cook for 1 to 2 minutes (be careful not to let it burn). Add the tomato paste, green beans or okra, and garlic. Stir it all together.

Add the beans, bean broth or water, tomato, salt, and pepper. Bring to a boil. Reduce heat and let it simmer for about 15 minutes.

Stir in the coconut milk and simmer for another 10 minutes. Serve over rice with yogurt on the side.

Day 2

Spinach with Garbanzo Beans

This goes together quickly! I like using frozen spinach in this dish since it is something I can keep on hand in the freezer. If you prefer fresh spinach, the amount in one of the bags of baby spinach should be about right. This is excellent when served with a crusty bread.

- 1 tablespoon healthy fat
- ½ teaspoon garlic powder (or use 4 fresh cloves, minced)
- 1 onion, diced
- 1 (10 ounce) box frozen chopped spinach, thawed and drained well
- 3 cups cooked garbanzo beans
- ½ teaspoon ground cumin
- ½ teaspoon sea salt
- ½ cup broth

In a skillet over medium heat, cook the garlic and onion in the healthy fat until translucent, about 5 minutes.

Add the spinach, garbanzo beans, cumin, salt, and broth. Mix well. Cook until heated through, lightly mashing the beans as it cooks. Taste and add additional salt and a little black pepper as desired.

Day 3

Chickpea Tacos

I found this recipe over a decade ago. I can't remember the original source and have changed it over time to better reflect our tastes. If avocado is out of your budget, you can omit it. It will still be delicious!

- 2 cups cooked garbanzo beans
- 1 avocado, chopped
- Fresh cilantro, to taste
- Juice of one lime (about 2 tablespoons)

- 1 clove garlic, minced
- Ground cumin, to taste
- Sea salt, to taste
- Black pepper, to taste
- 2 cups rice, cooked and seasoned with salt and pepper (or done Spanish style*)
- 2 cups salad greens
- Toppers, such as sour cream, salsa, shredded cheese, etc.
- Tortillas (sourdough, flour, or corn)

In a bowl, mash the avocado, then stir in the garbanzo beans, cilantro, garlic, and lime juice. Add cumin, salt, and pepper to taste.

Assemble the tacos with the garbanzo bean mixture, salad greens, rice, and your choice of toppers.

*Spanish-style rice: To 2 cups cooked rice, add 1 cup of salsa, ½ teaspoon sea salt, ¼ teaspoon black pepper, and 1 tablespoon lime.

Meal Options 2

- Easy Garbanzo Beans and Rice
- Garbanzo Bean and Sprouted Wheat Dish
- Hummus Platter

Do you like hummus? Once you make it from scratch, you'll never want to buy hummus again. And it's so easy! We like to keep Friday nights fun and festive, so I plan my Day 3 meal to fall on this night. Hummus, tzatziki, slices of cucumber, olives, cheeses, dried fruit, nuts, pita wedges and/or crackers along with tiny minty meatballs (to be eaten off of a toothpick) make for an almost celebratory meal.

You'll need 4 cups of beans for Day 1, 3 cups for Day 2, and 2 cups for Day 3. Any leftover beans can be frozen in 1-cup containers for later use or served for lunches during the week. Save ½ cup aquafaba for the Day 3 hummus.

Day 1

Easy Garbanzo Beans and Rice

This is a good one! My favorite way to serve this may sound a little strange: a scoop of rice, a big ladleful of beans (making sure to capture some of the broth), then topped with a mixed green salad. The lettuce wilts slightly and everything just seems to work. Sautéed zucchini is also an excellent topper in place of the mixed greens.

- 2 teaspoons healthy fat
- 1 onion, minced
- ½ teaspoon garlic powder (or 4 cloves fresh garlic, minced)
- 3 tablespoons fresh ginger, peeled and finely grated (or ¾ teaspoon ground ginger)
- 1 tablespoon ground cumin
- 2 teaspoons ground coriander
- 1 teaspoon ground turmeric
- ¼ teaspoon cayenne pepper
- 1 cup fresh or canned tomato sauce

- 1 cup broth (any variety, including the broth from cooking the beans)
- 4 cups cooked chickpeas, drained and rinsed
- 1 tablespoon lemon juice
- Sea salt, to taste
- Black pepper, to taste

Heat the fat in a skillet over medium-high heat. Sauté onions until translucent and soft. Turn down heat and add garlic, ginger, cumin, coriander, turmeric, and cayenne pepper. Sauté, stirring constantly, until everything is well combined and the mixture has a uniform color, about two minutes.

Stir in the tomato juice and broth, turn the heat up to medium, and bring to a gentle simmer. Add the chickpeas and return to a simmer. Cover, reduce the heat to low, and simmer until the mixture is thick (about 20 minutes). You can add additional broth, bean water, or plain water to maintain some juice.

Stir in the lemon juice and remove from the heat. Let the chickpeas sit 10 minutes before serving over rice.

Day 2

Garbanzo Bean and Sprouted Wheat Dish

Sprouted wheat makes a wonderful alternative to the common beans and rice. The original recipe called for bulgur. If you prefer not to take the time to sprout wheat, feel free to use bulgur.

- ¾ pounds stew meat (optional; lamb, antelope, venison, beef, etc.)
- 1 onion, chopped
- Sea salt, to taste
- Black pepper, to taste
- 4 cups cooked garbanzo beans
- 2 tablespoons healthy fat
- 2 cups sprouted wheat
- 1 tablespoon fresh mint, chopped (or ½ teaspoon dried mint)
- Yogurt

If using meat, put it in a saucepan and cover with water. Season with salt, cover with a lid, and simmer for 45 minutes to 1 hour until the meat is tender.

In a cast iron skillet, gently melt the butter and then add the sprouted wheat and lightly toast it.

Add the garbanzo beans, onions, salt, pepper, and toasted sprouts to the stew meat. If using dried mint, add it now. Simmer for 10 minutes to allow the flavors to meld. If using fresh mint, add at the end of cooking time.

Serve topped with yogurt.

Day 3

Hummus Platter

While I love hummus with tahini, sometimes my budget can't stretch far enough for the cost of tahini. This tahini-free hummus is still a tasty treat. Make the tzatziki first to allow the flavors to blend while assembling everything else.

Hummus

- 2 cups garbanzo beans, cooked and drained
- ¼ cup olive oil (mild)
- 1 tablespoon lemon juice
- 2 cloves fresh garlic (you can use ¼ teaspoon garlic powder, but fresh is best)
- ¼ cup aquafaba (bean cooking liquid) or pure water

Put all ingredients, except aquafaba, in a food processor or blender. Blend to make a smooth paste. Add the aquafaba a little at a time to achieve desired consistency.

When serving, drizzle with additional olive oil and a dash of paprika. On a large platter (or in individual bowls), put a mound of hummus, tzatziki, cucumber slices, olives, cheeses, dried fruit, nuts, pita wedges and/or crackers along with tiny minty meatballs.

Easy Tzatziki

- ½ cucumber, peeled, seeded, and grated
- 1 cup yogurt
- 1 tablespoon lemon juice
- 1 tablespoon fresh dill, minced (or 1 teaspoon dried dill)
- 1 clove garlic, minced
- Sea salt, to taste
- Black pepper, to taste

Mix all ingredients in a bowl. Chill for at least half an hour before serving.

Lentils

My first sampling of lentils was in a soup at a special dinner I went to in a Moroccan restaurant in Northwest Portland. It was a fabulous five-course meal, with the soup being the first course, and an incredibly fun event. I loved the soup so much, I begged for the recipe. They didn't share it, but I was able to find a reasonable facsimile on the internet. You'll find this recipe in Meal Options 3.

When I started working with lentils at home, specifically in my Stretchy Bean efforts, I would cook the beans in the same manner as pinto or black beans, then use the cooked beans in multiple dishes. While this works fine, lentils don't hold up well when reheating. This means only certain recipes are really appropriate past Day 1 if you don't want a mushy, semi-congealed mess. Yeah, that doesn't sound very appetizing!

My preference now, as opposed to cooking, is sprouting. Lentils taste wonderful when sprouted and maintain their shape beautifully. I love the slight crispness a sprouted lentil has, plus sprouting increases nutrition and makes them even more digestible than soaking alone. Remember, you can sprout any legume before cooking if you find soaking doesn't eliminate a good portion of the undesired side effects beans and legumes are famous for. If you choose to sprout kidney beans, be sure to follow with proper and safe cooking procedures.

There are several varieties of lentils. I prefer the common variety: brown lentils. They are widely available and extremely economical. The neutral flavor lends well to a variety of dishes spanning ethnicities. I'm such a fan of the simple lentil that, when

I work out of town, I sprout a batch of lentils for my meals during the week. When we took a family trip to the Grand Canyon, where the hotel rooms do not allow cooking, we feasted on sprouted lentil salads. You can read more about how we take lentils on the road in my book *Real Food Hits the Road*.

Sprouted Lentils

The night before Day 1, clean and rinse your lentils. Then put them in a large stockpot or bowl and cover with fresh water. In the morning, drain the lentils into a large colander. Rinse with fresh water and give them a good shake. Place the colander on a plate and cover with a towel. About an hour before you're ready to make your meal, remove the amount of lentils needed for Day 1. Leave the rest of the lentils in the colander.

Follow the chapter on sprouting for instructions on rinsing. You'll remove the amount of needed lentils on the appropriate days, allowing the remaining legumes to continue the sprouting process.

Meal Options 1

- Mujadareh
- Garam Masala Lentil Soup
- Lentils and Sweet Potatoes

These are all very warming and comforting dishes, perfect for a fall or winter evening. Be sure to refer to the chapter on sprouting legumes for additional details.

You'll need 6 cups of spouted lentils for Day 1, 2 cups for Day 2, and 3 cups for Day 3. Because the lentils expand while sprouting, you will likely have leftovers. They can be frozen for future use in soups, stews, burgers, or a hummus-like dish. Or use the leftover sprouted lentils to make a delicious salad.

Day 1

Mujadareh

This is one of my favorite dishes. My friend Wardee, from Traditional Cooking School, shares her traditional recipe for Mujadareh. I've made just enough tweaks to accommodate for my Stretchy Bean needs, so it's no longer traditional. But it's still delicious! I make an extra-large batch of this since it is my favorite. It tastes even better the next day for lunch. If you don't like the idea of eating lentils for so many meals, you can cut the recipe in half.

We like to serve this with a green salad dressed simply with vinegar and oil.

- 1 cup brown rice, uncooked*
- 1 tablespoon raw apple cider vinegar, lemon juice, or whey
- 8 to 12 cups water, divided
- 6 cups lentils, soaked and sprouted for the day
- 2 large onions, sliced
- 4 tablespoons healthy fat
- Sea salt, to taste
- Black pepper, to taste
- Cinnamon, to taste (optional)

In the morning, put rice and apple cider vinegar in a bowl or stockpot. Cover with fresh water, more than an inch above the rice. Leave on the countertop, covered with a cloth, for the day until you're ready to cook dinner.

Drain the rice and then add it to a large stockpot with 5 cups of lentils and 8 cups of water (or 4 cups broth and 4 cups of water). Bring to a boil. Reduce heat, then cover and simmer for 30 to 40 minutes until the rice and lentils are soft and the water has evaporated.

While the lentils and rice are cooking, sauté the onions in fat in a separate skillet until they are soft and caramelized (about 20 to 30 minutes). As the onion is cooking, sprinkle them a few times with sea salt. Remove from heat. Transfer onions to a blender and puree until smooth. Alternately, you can use a potato masher and mash to a chunky consistency. Sometimes I don't bother with this and just leave them whole.

Add the pureed (or not) onions to the cooked lentils and rice and simmer for 5 minutes, stirring occasionally. Taste and add salt, pepper, and cinnamon as desired.

Alternate method: I often make this dish using leftover cooked rice. For this method, skip the step of soaking the rice. Instead of adding the rice to the lentils for cooking, allow the lentils to cook until almost soft (25 to 35 minutes), then add the cooked rice. Stir to mix and cook for 5 additional minutes.

With this method, I reduce the broth for cooking the lentils to 6 cups. You may need to add a small amount of additional broth as the dish cooks. The finished version should not be a soup consistency, it is more of a casserole.

Day 2

Garam Masala Lentil Soup

I've been making this recipe for a dozen years. Even so, every time the flavor makes me say, *"Mmmmmm."* It is truly amazing. I've adapted it slightly from the original recipe shared by The Nourishing Gourmet to allow for the lightly sprouted lentils.

The tadka, a combination of spices resulting in a homemade Garam Masala, is the perfect finishing touch when combined with the coconut milk. When I first started making this dish, I couldn't fit the individual spices into my budget, so I purchased an already combined Garam Masala. It was still delicious! Serve with an extra dash of nutmeg on each bowl.

- 1 cup brown rice
- 1 tablespoon raw apple cider vinegar, lemon juice, or whey
- 4 cups water (approximate amount for soaking rice)
- 2 tablespoons healthy fat
- 1 onion, finely chopped
- ½ teaspoon turmeric
- 3 garlic cloves, finely chopped (or use about ½ teaspoon garlic powder)
- 8 cups of broth, water, or a combination
- 2 cups lentils, soaked and lightly sprouted
- 1 (14 ounce) can of coconut milk
- Sea salt, to taste

Tadka*

- ¼ cup healthy fat
- ¾ teaspoon ground cardamom

- ¼ teaspoon cinnamon
- ¼ teaspoon cloves
- ¼ black pepper
- ⅛ teaspoon fresh nutmeg, grated

In the morning, put the rice and apple cider vinegar in a bowl or stockpot. Cover with fresh water, more than an inch above the rice. Leave on the countertop, covered with a cloth, for the day. Drain and rinse (if desired) before beginning the cooking process.

Heat the healthy fat in a large soup pot over medium heat. Sauté the onions until they begin to soften, about 5 minutes. Add the turmeric. Cook and stir for another minute.

Stir in the garlic, swishing around to coat with fat and turmeric. Add broth or water, lentils, and rice. Simmer on low for about 30 minutes until the lentils and rice are soft and cooked through.

Puree the soup with an immersion blender (or in a standard blender) to your desired consistency.

To make the tadka, melt the healthy fat in a small saucepan. Add the spices and stir consistently, to prevent burning, for about 1 minute.

Whisk the tadka and coconut milk into the soup. Taste for seasoning, adding additional sea salt if needed. Return to a low simmer to heat through before serving.

*Tadka: If you can't fit the individual spices into your budget, commercially available Garam Masala seasoning works just fine—use 1 ½ teaspoons. You may need to add additional black pepper when you taste for seasoning. The Garam Masala can also be added via a shaker to individual bowls. Yum!

Day 3

Lentils and Sweet Potatoes

Sprouted lentils provide amazing versatility! The sprouted lentils combined with sweet potatoes make a wonderful combination.

- Sweet potatoes (½ to 1 per person, based on size and individual appetites)
- 3 cups sprouted lentils
- 2 tablespoons healthy fat
- 1 onion, diced
- 1 teaspoon ground cumin
- ½ teaspoon garlic powder
- 1 teaspoon ground ginger
- ¼ teaspoon ground cinnamon
- ½ teaspoon sweet paprika
- 1 teaspoon ground chili powder
- ½ teaspoon sea salt
- 1 (15 ounce) can diced tomatoes, drained
- 4 cups firmly packed baby spinach
- ¼ to 1 cup broth, water, or a combination of both
- Toppers such as sour cream and/or cilantro

Bake the sweet potatoes until soft.

Steam the sprouted lentils for about 3 minutes until they are al dente, then place in a bowl and set aside.

Heat the oil in a large skillet over medium heat, then add the onions and sauté until translucent. Add the spices and stir to combine. Add tomatoes and cook, stirring frequently until mixed.

Decrease the heat to low and stir in the lentils and spinach. Cook, stirring frequently, until the spinach has wilted, adding broth by the ¼ cup if needed to prevent sticking (about 1 to 2 minutes). Taste to adjust seasonings as desired.

Split the sweet potatoes in half and use a fork to coarsely mash the flesh, leaving it in the skin. To serve, place the sweet potato halves on each serving plate and top with a generous scoop of lentils. Serve right away, topped with a dollop of sour cream and torn cilantro leaves.

Meal Options 2

- Smokey Lentils and Rice
- Sprouted Lentil Tacos
- Sprouted Lentil Patties

This rotation of meals is one of my summer favorites. The minimal cooking keeps the kitchen cool, while still providing hearty dishes. As mentioned in the Meal Options 1 section, refer to the chapter on sprouting legumes for additional details.

You'll need 3 cups of sprouted lentils for Day 1, 3 cups for Day 2, and 4 cups for Day 3. Because the lentils expand while sprouting, you will likely have leftovers. They can be frozen for future use in soups, stews, burgers, or a hummus-like dish. Or use the leftover sprouted lentils to make a delicious salad.

Day 1

Smokey Lentils and Rice

Last summer, when looking for a new lentil dish, I stumbled across this recipe and was especially drawn to it for two reasons.

One, the original instructions called for cooking in the Instant Pot, which is perfect for summer so the kitchen doesn't have extra heat added to it. While I do love using my Instant Pot, I've found this recipe works just as well on the stovetop, without taking much additional time, and that's my preferred cooking method.

Two, it uses smoked paprika. I have an extreme fondness for smoked paprika! Smoked paprika comes from chilies that are smoked, dried, and crushed. Regular paprika doesn't use the smoking process. If you can't fit smoked paprika into your budget, you can use regular paprika plus a dash or two of liquid smoke (if this is something you keep in your cupboard).

- 2 cups brown rice
- 2 tablespoons raw apple cider vinegar, lemon juice, or whey
- 4 cups pure water (approximate amount for soaking rice)
- 3 cups lentils, soaked and sprouted for the day
- 6 cups broth, water, or a combination of the two
- 2 tablespoons onion, finely minced
- 2 tablespoons smoked paprika
- 1 teaspoon garlic powder
- 1 teaspoon black pepper
- 1 teaspoon sea salt
- 1 tablespoon apple cider vinegar

In the morning, put rice and apple cider vinegar in a bowl or stockpot. Cover with fresh water, at least an inch above the rice. Leave on the countertop, covered with a cloth, for the day.

When you're ready to prepare dinner, drain and rinse the rice (if desired). Place rice, lentils, broth, onion, smoked paprika*, and other spices in a large soup pot (do not add vinegar at this time). Bring to a boil, skimming if necessary.

Allow to boil for 5 minutes, stirring occasionally, then turn the heat down to a low simmer. Give it a stir every few minutes. Cook until the rice and lentils are soft and most of the liquid is absorbed (around 30 minutes).

Stir in apple cider vinegar. Turn off the heat and let sit, covered, for 5 minutes. Add additional salt and pepper as needed.

This is excellent served over salad greens and topped with salsa and sour cream. Another fun option is to use this as a nacho topping served over tortilla chips.

*If you're using regular paprika and liquid smoke, add the liquid smoke when adding the vinegar.

Day 2

Sprouted Lentil Tacos

This is another great recipe from Traditional Cooking School. I've made some minor adaptions to it, including adding a small amount of broth to increase nutrition.

- 1 onion, diced
- Healthy fat
- ¼ teaspoon garlic powder
- 1 teaspoon chili powder (use more if you prefer a spicier dish)
- Pinch of red pepper flakes
- Dash of paprika (smoked or regular; I love the smoked)
- 1 teaspoon ground cumin
- ¼ teaspoon dried oregano
- ¼ teaspoon black pepper
- 3 cups lentils, sprouted at least 2 days
- ¼ cup broth or water
- Sea salt, to taste
- Tortillas (sourdough, flour, or corn)
- Toppers, such as shredded cheese, diced avocado, cilantro, salsa, etc.

Steam the sprouted lentils for about 5 minutes.

While the lentils are steaming, sauté the onion in healthy fat. When they become soft, add the spices and stir to coat the onions. Add the steamed lentils and the broth. Stir and let the broth evaporate slightly, allowing the flavors to combine.

Assemble tacos with lentils and desired toppers.

Day 3

Sprouted Lentil Patties

These burgers take a few minutes to put together but are very much worth the effort! Use your fully sprouted lentils in this dish. These patties are very fragile, and while they could be used as a burger, we prefer them as a patty—to be eaten with a fork—with a salad on the side.

These are wonderful served with a tahini dressing. Unfortunately, tahini isn't something I can always fit in my budget. A good alternative is tzatziki (this recipe is shared in the Garbanzo Bean section under Hummus Platter).

- 4 cups sprouted lentils, divided
- 3 cloves garlic, peeled (or ½ teaspoon garlic powder)
- 1 teaspoon horseradish, grated (fresh or from a jar)
- 1 inch ginger root, peeled (or use 1 teaspoon ground ginger)
- 1 teaspoon sea salt
- ¼ cup healthy fat (for patties)
- 2 tablespoons healthy fat (for frying)

In a skillet, heat up 2 tablespoons of healthy fat over medium heat.

In a blender or food processor, puree 1 cup of lentils, ¼ cup of healthy fat (coconut oil or palm oil are wonderful; olive oil will also work), garlic, horseradish, ginger, and salt. Add the remaining lentils and pulse until coarsely chopped while still retaining some texture.

Using your hands, form the lentil mixture into patties. Add the patties to the skillet and fry until golden brown, then flip and repeat on the other side.

Serve on hamburger buns or in a lettuce wrap, topped with tomatoes, cheese, onion, etc.

Meal Options 3

- Moroccan Lentil Soup
- Marinated Lentils
- Sprouted Lentil Bibimbap

This rotation begins with a similar replica to my first lentil experience. Be sure to refer to the chapter on sprouting legumes for additional details.

You'll need 4 cups of sprouted lentils for Day 1, 3 cups for Day 2, and 3 cups for Day 3. Because the lentils expand while sprouting, you will likely have leftovers. They can be frozen for future use in soups, stews, burgers, or a hummus-like dish. Or use the leftover sprouted lentils to make a delicious salad.

Day 1

Moroccan Lentil Soup

While not an exact replica of the lentil soup I fell in love with, it's very reminiscent of it and tastes delicious. If you use broth in making the soup, it needs to be a mild broth, such as chicken or vegetable. Beef and wild game broth are too strong for this dish. Serve with crusty bread.

- 2 large onions, chopped
- 2 tablespoons healthy fat
- 1 teaspoon ground cumin
- ¼ teaspoon garlic powder
- 4 cups lentils, soaked and sprouted for the day
- 7 cups broth, water, or a combination; divided
- 1 cup tomato sauce
- 1 teaspoon paprika
- 1 tablespoon dried parsley, crushed (or use ¼ cup fresh parsley)
- ½ teaspoon black pepper
- 1 teaspoon sea salt (or to taste)

In a large stockpot, sauté onions in fat until translucent. Add cumin and garlic powder, giving a quick stir. Add lentils and 5 cups of broth. Bring to a boil, skimming if necessary. Let boil for a couple of minutes, then reduce heat to a simmer. Simmer for about 30 minutes until the lentils are slightly soft.

Add the additional 2 cups of broth and stir. Mix in tomato sauce and remaining seasonings. Lower the heat and simmer for an additional 10 minutes. When serving, add a drizzle of olive oil to each bowl.

Day 2

Marinated Lentils

These are incredibly versatile. A little like a salad, you can use them as a topper for greens, stuff them in a pita shell or wrap, or eat them as is. This dish is best made in advance. It's easy to mix it up the night before or the morning of. The longer it sets, the more time the flavors have to develop. But you can, of course, mix it up and serve immediately and it will still be great!

- 3 tablespoons extra-virgin olive oil
- 2 ½ tablespoons red wine vinegar (or to taste)
- 1 tablespoon lemon juice
- 1 ½ teaspoons mustard
- 1 ½ teaspoons pure maple syrup, honey, or granulated sugar
- 1 teaspoon sea salt (or to taste)
- ¼ teaspoon black pepper
- 1 to 1 ½ cups green onions (about 1 bunch), thinly sliced, dark and light green parts
- ⅓ cup fresh parsley, minced*
- 1 cup tomatoes, diced (fresh or canned, well drained)
- 3 cups lentils, sprouted at least 2 days

In a large bowl, whisk together the oil, vinegar, lemon juice, mustard, sweetener, salt, and pepper. Stir in the green onions, parsley, tomatoes, and lentil sprouts. Season with additional salt and pepper to taste.

*Fresh parsley is best in this recipe, but you can also use dried parsley that is rehydrated and well drained.

Day 3

Sprouted Lentil Bibimbap

I'll admit, I'm taking a lot of liberties by referring to this as the Bibimbap. Bibimbap, the traditional Korean dish, translates to "mixed rice with meat and assorted vegetables." There's no meat in this dish, so I've immediately strayed from tradition. However, the beautifully flavored lentils make a nice substitute.

This dish is incredibly flexible, allowing you to use ingredients you have on hand. There is a lot going on with this dish, but it comes together easily. I list many options for fresh and sautéed vegetables. You don't have to use them all. This is a great dish for cleaning up odds and ends from the fridge.

To really make this dish amazing, consider starting a batch of kimchi the week before. Kimchi is a classic Korean sauerkraut with amazing flavors and a bit of a kick.

Lentils and Sauce

- 3 cups lentils, sprouted with a tail
- 2 tablespoons soy sauce
- 2 tablespoons sesame oil (use olive oil if you don't have sesame)
- 1 teaspoon Sucanat
- ¼ teaspoon garlic powder
- 2 teaspoons healthy fat

Sautéed Spinach

- 2 teaspoons healthy fat

- 6 cups fresh spinach, loosely packed
- 1 teaspoon sesame oil (or olive oil)
- Pinch of sea salt

Sautéed Vegetables (Use Some or All)

- 2 teaspoons healthy fat
- 1 carrot, cut into short thin strips (julienned)
- 1 zucchini, cut into short thin strips
- 2 green onions, sliced
- ½ bell pepper (any color), cut into thin strips
- ¼ pound mushrooms, sliced (or julienne if you prefer conformity)
- 1 or 2 cups cabbage, sliced very thin
- Pinch of sea salt

Fresh Vegetables (Use Some or All)

- 2 green onions, sliced
- 1 cucumber, cut into short thin strips
- ½ bell pepper, cut into short thin strips
- Kimchi

Additional

- 1 or 2 eggs per person
- Steamed rice, still warm
- Sauces such as soy sauce, Sriracha, or chili garlic sauce
- Sesame seeds for garnish

Lentils and Sauce

Marinate the lentils in all ingredients except the healthy fat for about 30 minutes to enhance the flavor while you are working on the other ingredients. If you haven't started your rice, start it now.

Clean, cut, and prepare all of your vegetables. I like to put everything in separate sections on a large cutting board or use little bowls.

Sautéed Spinach

Heat a large skillet over medium heat and add the fat. Spread the fat evenly over the pan, then add the spinach. Stir to coat. Sauté just until it is wilted, about 3 minutes. Turn off the heat. Drizzle with sesame oil and season with salt. Remove the spinach from the skillet and place in a clean bowl.

Sautéed Vegetables

Using the same skillet you sautéed the spinach in, add fat over medium heat. Spread evenly and then add your chosen vegetables. Cook until the vegetables begin to soften, seasoning with sea salt as they cook. You may need to add a little water, a teaspoon at a time, to help with the cooking process. Since the vegetables are thinly sliced, it should only take a few minutes. Remove the vegetables from the skillet and place in a clean bowl.

Lentils and Sauce

Now that the lentils have marinated, put the healthy fat in the skillet you used for the spinach and vegetables over medium heat. Spread evenly, then add the lentils and sauce. Sauté, stirring continually, until the lentils soften (about 3 to 5 minutes). Remove lentils from the skillet and place in a clean bowl.

Eggs

Fry or poach the eggs to your desired consistency.

Assemble

This is the fun part! Each bowl can be built to the individual's specification. Start with rice (½ to 1 cup, depending on appetite). Then add the spinach, cooked veggies, and cooked lentils. Top with raw veggies and/or kimchi. Put an egg over the top of it all. Finish with sauce and a sprinkle of sesame seeds.

Meal Options 4

- Friar's Lentil Soup
- Lentils and Dumplings
- Creamy Lenticchie

This rotation is all about soup! I'll admit, I thought my husband might balk about three nights of lentil soup, but each dish brings its own flavor and each is truly amazing.

You'll need 4 cups of sprouted lentils for Day 1, 3 cups for Day 2, and 3 cups for Day 3. Because the lentils expand while sprouting, you'll likely have leftovers. They can be frozen for future use in soups, stews, burgers, or a hummus-like dish. Or use the leftover sprouted lentils to make a delicious salad.

Day 1

Friar's Lentil Soup

I found this tasty recipe in the cookbook *Family, Food and the Friars* by Geno Barbaro. The combination of the vegetables and lentils makes a very satisfying dish. When I'm working out of town, I often make this on the first night I'm there so that I have lunches all week. This soup is delicious when served with a sprinkle of Parmesan cheese and crusty bread.

- 2 tablespoons healthy fat
- 1 small to medium onion, diced
- 1 celery stalk, diced
- 1 carrot, peeled and diced
- 1 medium potato, diced
- ¼ teaspoon garlic powder (or 2 cloves fresh garlic, minced)
- 4 cups lentils, soaked and sprouted for the day
- 7 cups broth, water, or a combination

Heat fat in a soup pot with the onion and celery until softened. Add carrot and potato, stirring to combine so it all has some of the fat on it. Stir in the garlic and lentils, combining again. Add broth and bring to a boil. Reduce heat to simmer and cook for 30 to 45 minutes until the lentils and vegetables are soft.

Day 2

Lentils and Dumplings

Dumplings! These delicious little pieces of dough steamed in broth make a wonderful, hearty addition to any soup, stew, or even chili. Oftentimes, I'll stretch the remainder of a pot of soup by adding more water or broth and then topping it with dumplings. The dumplings give it extra heartiness and create an almost new experience. This is modified from a recipe on Hillbilly Housewife.

Soup

- 4 carrots, peeled and diced
- 3 or 4 celery stalks, diced
- 1 large onion, diced
- 2 tablespoons healthy fat
- 3 cups lentils, soaked and lightly sprouted
- 8 cups broth, water, or a combination of both
- 1 cup corn, canned or frozen (optional)
- 1 teaspoon sea salt
- 1 teaspoon garlic powder
- ¼ teaspoon black pepper

Dumplings

- 2 tablespoons melted butter or mild olive oil (or any healthy fat, melted)
- 1 egg (or 3 tablespoons more milk*)
- ½ cup milk
- 1 ½ cups flour
- 1 ½ teaspoons baking powder
- ½ teaspoon sea salt

- ½ teaspoon sugar

In a large soup pot, sauté the carrots, celery, and onion in the healthy fat for about 5 minutes until they begin to soften. Add the sprouted lentils and broth. Bring the mixture to a boil and simmer for 20 minutes.

Add corn (optional) and seasonings. Simmer for an additional 5 minutes while you mix up the dumplings.

Make the dumpling dough by combining melted butter, egg, and milk. In a separate bowl, mix the flour, baking powder, salt, and sugar. Add the dry ingredients to the wet, mixing until just combined.

Taste the soup for salt and pepper. Now evaluate the soup—it needs to be at a low simmer and needs enough liquid to well cover the veggies and lentils. When you add the dumplings, you'll leave the soup covered for 20 minutes to steam the dumplings, and the flour in the dumplings will thicken the broth. I like to make sure there's about two inches of liquid covering the solids.

Once you have it how you like it, add the dumplings. Drop the dough by the teaspoon into the simmering soup mixture. Cover and cook for 20 minutes. Don't take off the lid during this time. The heat from the hot soup and the steam results in lovely tender dumplings. When time is up, remove from heat and serve immediately. Make sure each bowl gets at least a dumpling or two to enjoy along with the soup. So good!

*If you're low on eggs, add the additional milk. The dumplings will have slightly less "fluff" but are still good.

Day 3

Creamy Lenticchie

There's something amazing about a creamy blended soup. When economical soup is a regular part of your diet, changing things up with an immersion blender and making a smooth puree is a welcome difference.

The first time I made this soup, from an internet recipe I stumbled across, it wasn't quite what I had in mind. While the flavors were good, the smoothness wasn't there. The addition of a potato and a small amount of cream turned something that was "fine" into something delicious. For a slightly different and dairy-free option, use the cream from a can of coconut milk. Serve with slices of thick, toasted garlic bread.

- 2 tablespoons healthy fat
- 1 onion, diced
- 1 carrot, diced
- 1 stalk of celery, diced
- 1 small potato, finely diced
- 3 cups lentils, fully sprouted with a tail
- 4 cups water
- Sea salt, to taste
- Black pepper, to taste
- ½ cup heavy cream (or the thick part of a can of full-fat coconut milk*)

In a soup pot, heat the fat over medium heat, then add the diced onion, carrot, celery, and potato. Sauté for 8 to 10 minutes, sprinkling with salt and pepper a few times during the cooking process.

Add the sprouted lentils and water. Bring to a boil, then reduce heat to simmer. Cook for 10 to 15 minutes until the lentils and vegetables are soft. Season with salt and pepper to taste. Remove from heat and add the cream.

Using an immersion blender, blend until smooth. Add additional boiling water, if needed, to arrive at the desired consistency.

Serve in individual bowls with a drizzle of olive oil and a dash of black pepper.

*If using canned coconut milk, set in the fridge for a couple of hours (up to 24 hours) so the cream thickens and separates from the milk. Open the can with a can opener and gently scrape off only the thick, creamy part. The rest of the coconut milk can be used in smoothies or other dishes.

Cooked Lentils

As already discussed, and evidenced by the multitude of recipes using sprouted lentils, my favorite way for using lentils is sprouting. Even so, there's still a spot in my repertoire for cooked lentils. Cooking gives a variation that is often welcome.

Meal Options

- Lentils and Rice
- Lentil Loaf
- Lentil and Rice Burgers

On the morning of Day 1, soak 1 pound of lentils and 1 pound of rice together in a large stockpot with a tight-fitting lid. Cover the lentils and rice with water, several inches over the top. If possible, check midday and add additional water. Follow the cooking directions in Day 1.

This will make enough lentils and rice for three meals. I remove the amounts needed for Day 2 and 3 before serving my Day 1 dish. You'll need 4 cups of the lentil and rice mixture for Day 2, and 3 cups for Day 3.

Day 1

Lentils and Rice

Lentils and rice cooked together and simply seasoned make not only a satisfying main dish but also work perfectly as a base for two additional meals. Use a big soup pot to cook the lentils and rice. As they soak and cook, they will expand.

We like to serve this over a mixed green salad, then top it with a simple vinaigrette. Or you could top it with hot sauce, cheese, sour cream, etc. and have the salad on the side. A nice crusty bread slathered in butter is the perfect accompaniment.

- Soaked lentils and rice (see instructions above for amount and soaking)
- 1 ½ teaspoon sea salt (plus additional to taste)
- Black pepper, to taste
- Toppers, such as hot sauce, shredded cheese, sour cream, etc.

About an hour before supper, drain the soaking water off the lentils and rice and replace it with 10 cups of fresh water. While I usually cook beans in broth to increase the nutrition, I prefer to cook this dish in pure water. Lentils are so mildly flavored that the broth can overpower the dish, and while this is fine for the Day 1 dish of lentils and rice, it doesn't work as well in the future dishes.

Bring to a boil, skimming as needed, then reduce the heat to a simmer. Cover and cook until the lentils and rice are tender and most of the liquid is absorbed (depending on different factors, this could take 30 minutes to 1 hour).

Turn off the heat and let stand for a few minutes to absorb any additional water. Stir in salt and pepper before serving.

Day 2

Lentil Loaf

While this lentil loaf does make a satisfying main dish, it is not a meatloaf. To prevent disappointment, don't try to pass it off as meatloaf. However, it does have a nice texture and a great flavor. When served with a green salad, it's a filling dish. While not too extensive, this dish does take a little more time and effort than most. Sautéing the vegetables and processing the lentils in advance shaves off a few minutes.

Loaf

- 2 tablespoons healthy fat
- 3 garlic cloves, minced
- 1 small onion, finely diced
- 1 small bell pepper (any color), finely diced
- 1 carrot, finely diced or grated
- 1 celery stalk, finely diced
- 1 teaspoon dried thyme
- ½ teaspoon ground cumin
- ½ teaspoon garlic powder
- ½ teaspoon onion powder
- ¼ to ½ teaspoon chili pepper (optional)
- 4 cups lentil and rice mixture
- 2 eggs
- Sea salt, to taste

- Black pepper, to taste
- ¾ cup oats
- ½ cup flour or finely ground oats

Glaze

- 3 tablespoons ketchup
- 1 tablespoon balsamic vinegar
- 1 tablespoon pure maple syrup or honey

Preheat oven to 350 degrees and grease a loaf pan.

Heat healthy fat over medium heat. Sauté the onion, garlic, bell pepper, carrot, and celery for about 5 minutes. Add all seasonings and mix well.

Mash up 3 cups of the lentil and rice mixture with a blender or food processor. (If you're making part of the recipe in advance, add the sautéed vegetables and the remaining unmashed lentils now and put in the refrigerator. Proceed with the recipe as written when ready to bake.)

In a bowl, combine the sautéed vegetables, egg, oats, flour, mashed lentil mixture, and remaining lentil mixture. Mix well. Salt, pepper, or add more seasonings to taste.

To make the glaze, combine all ingredients and mix well.

Press the mixture into the loaf pan and spread the glaze evenly over the top. Bake 45 to 50 minutes.

Day 3

Lentil and Rice Burgers

The combination of lentils and rice make these a hearty patty that's perfect for turning into a classically inspired burger. Sourdough English muffins make delicious buns (or use your favorite homemade or store-bought ones), then top with mayonnaise, ketchup, sliced red onion, and dill pickles. Yum!

- ½ to 1 onion, minced
- ½ to 1 bell pepper (any color), diced
- Healthy fat
- 3 cups lentil and rice mixture
- 2 eggs
- ½ cup flour
- 1 cup breadcrumbs (from any type of bread)
- ½ teaspoon chili powder
- ½ teaspoon garlic powder
- 1 teaspoon ground cumin
- ½ teaspoon smoked or regular paprika
- Sea salt, to taste
- Black pepper, to taste
- English muffins or hamburger buns
- Burger toppers, such as cheese, tomatoes, onion, lettuce, etc.

Preheat oven to 375 degrees. Cover a baking sheet with parchment paper.

Sauté the onion and pepper in a healthy fat until soft. Using a whole onion and pepper will result in a slightly larger quantity. If you need to stretch this further, feel free to add minced celery and/or minced or shredded carrots to the onion and pepper.

Meanwhile, puree ¾ of the lentil and rice mixture and the breadcrumbs with an immersion blender, standard blender, food processor, or potato masher. Add eggs and mix well, then add the remaining ¼ of the lentil and rice mixture along with the flour. Stir in the cooked veggies and seasonings.

Now you need to evaluate the texture. Is it thick enough to hold together? If not, stir in additional flour by the tablespoon. Is it too thick? You can add water by the tablespoon or an additional egg. You want a consistency that will hold together when you form the patties.

Using your hands, gently press into burger-sized patties and place on the baking sheet. Bake until firm (about 15 minutes) and then flip the patties over and bake an additional 7 to 10 minutes.

Serve with buns and fixings, just like a hamburger.

Whole and Split Peas

I first became interested in sprouting in late 2011. I started small with a few seeds but soon realized there was a whole wealth of items that could be sprouted. A friend shared her love of sprouting whole peas, and I soon jumped on that bandwagon! In early 2012, I was able to purchase 25 pounds of whole peas for $8.05. At 32 cents a pound, whole peas became my favorite Stretchy Bean.

The cost has crept up over the years. As I'm writing this, Azure Standard has whole peas at $22.02 for 25 pounds (88 cents per pound). Split peas, the same item but split in half, are 74 cents a pound when purchased in 25-pound bags. Out of all the beans and legumes offered by Azure Standard, split peas are the least expensive, with whole peas being a close second.

While green split peas are widely available in every grocery store, I've yet to see whole peas. Feel free to use green split peas in place of whole peas in any of these recipes. Will they sprout? Maybe, maybe not. I was always under the impression split peas could not be sprouted. And I've yet to be successful with creating a full tail on split peas, but I've had the beginning of partial sprouts.

Even though I've yet to have tails produced from my split peas, I still go through the sprouting process, assuming I'm getting the nutritional benefits of sprouts. Keep in mind, whole peas will take longer to cook than split peas. Adjust your times accordingly.

Because both the whole and the split peas fall apart so readily with the cooking process, I've not found a way to cook a large batch to use in multiple meals. My preference for peas is to soak and sprout (or attempt to sprout). When using split peas, I am extra diligent with rinsing and often give an addition rinse midday.

Be sure to refer to the chapter on sprouting legumes for additional details. The night before Day 1, clean and rinse your peas. Then put them in a large stockpot or bowl and cover with fresh water. In the morning, drain into a large colander. Rinse with fresh water and give them a good shake. Place the colander on a plate and cover with a towel.

About an hour before you're ready to make your meal, remove the amount of peas needed for Day 1. Leave the rest in the colander. Follow the chapter on sprouting for instructions on rinsing. You'll remove the amount of needed peas on the appropriate days, allowing the remaining legumes to continue the sprouting process.

Meal Options 1

- Whole (or Split) Pea Soup
- Sprouted Pea Egg Foo Yung
- Sprouted Pea Salad

Not only are dried peas inexpensive, they are also folate- and fiber-rich in addition to being tasty. This rotation includes soup, salad, and Egg Foo Yung. Such variety!

You'll need 3 cups of soaked peas for Day 1, 2 cups for Day 2, and 3 cups for Day 3. Because the whole peas expand while sprouting, you may have leftovers. You could make an extra-large salad on Day 3 to accommodate for these and give you future lunches. Or they can be frozen for future use in soups, stews, burgers, or a hummus-like dish.

Day 1

Whole (or Split) Pea Soup

This delicious soup was originally written for split mung beans, but the whole or split peas work very well. I've also used lentils with excellent results. Serve this tasty soup with a crusty bread.

- 3 tablespoons healthy fat
- 1 onion, diced
- ½ teaspoon garlic powder (or 3 to 4 cloves fresh garlic, minced)
- 1 teaspoon ground turmeric
- ¾ teaspoon ground cumin
- ¼ teaspoon dried ginger
- 8 cups broth, water, or a combination; divided
- 3 cups whole or split peas, soaked and sprouted for the day
- 1 medium tomato, diced
- 3 teaspoons sea salt (or to taste)

In a large soup pot, sauté the onions in the fat. When the onions are soft, stir in the garlic, turmeric, cumin, and ginger. Add about 1 cup of broth and stir well, then add the peas and remaining broth. Bring to a boil, skimming as necessary.

Turn down the heat and simmer until the peas are soft and the soup begins to thicken. Remember, whole peas take longer to cook than split peas. Whole peas that have been soaked take 45 minutes to 1 hour. Split peas take about 30 minutes.

Add the diced tomatoes, then salt and pepper to taste. Allow to simmer an additional 5 minutes before serving.

Day 2

Sprouted Pea Egg Foo Yung

For several years, these economical pancakes were a mainstay in our house. The flavor is very reminiscent of dining out, but at a fraction of the cost.

Egg Pancakes

- 3 or 4 green onions, trimmed and cut however you like
- ¼ cup celery, finely diced
- 5 eggs
- ½ cup milk or water
- ½ teaspoon sea salt
- Black pepper, to taste
- 3 cups whole or split peas, soaked and lightly sprouted
- Healthy fat

Gravy

- ½ cup flour
- ½ cup water
- 2 cups broth
- ¼ cup tamari or soy sauce
- Sea salt, to taste

- Black pepper, to taste

Beat the eggs, then add milk or water and mix well. Stir in the vegetables, salt, pepper, and peas.

Using a cast iron or similar skillet, heat a little healthy fat (I like to use ghee or coconut oil for this). These cook like pancakes. Put a small amount of the batter in your pan. Allow to cook for a couple of minutes on one side and then gently flip to cook on the other side. Continue until all are cooked.

Meanwhile, make the gravy by bringing broth to a boil. Combine the flour and water into a paste, then whisk it into the boiling broth. Be sure to whisk well to avoid lumps. Once your gravy is thick, add tamari and then salt and pepper. Taste and adjust seasonings as needed.

To serve, top the egg pancakes with gravy. We like to serve these with rice and extra gravy.

Day 3

Sprouted Pea Salad

This is a wonderful way to use up odds and ends of fresh vegetables. Whatever you have in your fridge is fair game for this delightful salad. I've modeled this after a sprouted lentil salad from Traditional Cooking School. You can also add meat, fish, hard-boiled and diced eggs, or just about anything else that sounds good to you.

- 4 cups sprouted whole or split peas

- ⅛ red or white onion, finely diced or thinly sliced
- ½ cup black olives, sliced
- Your choice of fresh vegetables, diced (such as tomatoes, peppers, cucumbers, avocado, etc.)
- 1 clove garlic, crushed (or ¼ teaspoon garlic powder)
- Cubed, shredded, or crumbled cheese (your choice of variety)
- ¼ cup olive oil (or avocado oil)
- 2 tablespoons balsamic vinegar, red wine, or rice wine vinegar
- ¼ to ½ teaspoon sea salt, plus more to taste
- Black pepper, to taste

Steam the sprouted peas. Whole peas need to steam for 25 to 30 minutes. Split peas will take 10 or less minutes. You want them soft but not falling apart. Allow to cool to room temperature.

Once they are cool, add in your vegetables, cheese, and meat (if using). Mix all together. Add your olive oil, vinegar, salt, and pepper. Stir gently. Taste and adjust seasonings as needed. You may need a little extra olive oil and/or vinegar depending on the amount of vegetables you've added.

Meal Options 2

- Blended Pea Soup
- Pea Curry
- Pea Pâté

Pea pâté? Doesn't it sound nearly decadent? This is something like a chickpea hummus but with a little more depth, thanks to sautéing the onions before blending. It's a delicious and versatile finish to this Stretchy Bean rotation.

You'll need 3 cups of soaked peas for Day 1, 2 cups for Day 2, and 3 cups for Day 3. Because the whole peas expand while sprouting, you may have leftovers. You could make an extra-large salad on Day 3 to accommodate for these and give you future lunches. Or they can be frozen for future use in soups, stews, burgers, or a hummus-like dish.

Day 1

Blended Pea Soup

This soup is adapted from the recipe for Pea Soup in the book *Nourishing Traditions* by Sally Fallon. The original recipe uses either freshly shelled or frozen peas and doesn't include the carrot. The addition of the carrots really seems to work well and increases the flavor. If you're not a fan of carrots, feel free to leave them out. Homemade croutons are an excellent topper on this soup.

- 2 medium onions, diced
- 2 carrots, diced
- 3 tablespoons healthy fat
- 4 cups whole or split peas, soaked and sprouted for the day
- 8 cups broth (chicken or vegetable is best)
- Sea salt, to taste

- Black pepper, to taste
- Sour cream or crème fraiche

In a large soup pot, sauté the onions and carrots in the fat until the onions are translucent. Add the peas and broth. Bring to a boil, skimming as needed. Reduce heat and simmer until the peas are soft (about 60 minutes for whole peas and 30 minutes for split peas). You may need to add additional broth or water during the simmering time.

When the peas are soft, puree with an immersion blender. Season to taste, then serve and top the individual bowls with sour cream.

Day 2

Pea Curry

This is a delicious, mild, and quick curry dish. Serve over rice with yogurt on the side.

- 2 tablespoons healthy fat
- 1 medium onion, diced
- 3 garlic cloves, minced
- 2 tablespoons fresh ginger (about 2 inches), peeled and grated (or ½ teaspoon ground ginger)
- 1 to 3 tablespoons curry powder
- 2 medium carrots, diced
- 1 (14 ounce) can diced tomatoes
- 2 cups broth
- 3 cups whole or split peas, soaked and lightly sprouted

- 1 can coconut milk
- Lemon juice, to taste
- Sea salt, to taste
- Black pepper, to taste

Heat healthy fat in a soup pot, then sauté the onion until it begins to soften.

Stir in the garlic, curry powder, and grated ginger. Add carrots, tomatoes, and peas. Stir to mix, then add the broth.

Bring to a boil and then cook half-covered over medium heat for around 30 to 60 minutes (less time for split peas than whole peas) until the peas are cooked and the vegetables are tender. Stir in the coconut milk. Season to taste with lemon juice, salt, and pepper.

Day 3

Pea Pâté

This pâté can be served on a platter (see Hummus Platter under the Garbanzo Bean section) or on a hearty, sturdy toast for an open-faced sandwich with a salad on the side.

- 2 cups sprouted whole or split peas
- 2 tablespoons healthy fat
- 1 medium onion, diced
- 1 clove garlic, diced (or ¼ teaspoon garlic powder)
- 1 ½ teaspoons lemon juice (about ½ a whole lemon)

- 2 tablespoons fresh parsley, snipped (or 2 teaspoons dried parsley)
- 2 tablespoons fresh chives, snipped (or 2 teaspoons dried chives)
- 1 to 3 tablespoons water
- Sea salt, to taste
- Black pepper, to taste

Steam the sprouted peas. Whole peas need to steam for 25 to 30 minutes. Split peas will take 10 minutes or less. You want them soft but not falling apart. Allow to cool to room temperature.

While the peas are cooling, sauté the onions in the fat until lightly browned. Add the garlic, stirring and cooking for another minute.

Put the steamed peas, onions, lemon juice, parsley, and chives in a food processor or blender (or you can put it all in a bowl and use a hand mixer). Blend until it's a smooth puree, adding 1 tablespoon of water at a time as needed to produce a smooth finish.

More From Millie Copper

Get 20% off Millie Copper's nonfiction eBooks at HomespunOasis.com/Books with coupon code SAVE20.

Real Food Hits the Road: Budget-Friendly Tips, Ideas, and Recipes for Enjoying Real Food Away from Home

Are you planning to hit the road for a family vacation? Do you want to take a road trip, but the idea of eating out three meals a day doesn't work for your budget or your health?

Real Food Hits the Road will be your guide to saving the budget, keeping your digestion working well, and eating real food away from home while letting you enjoy the trip and not "cook" all of the time.

Stock the Real Food Pantry: Save Money and Time While Gaining Peace of Mind

Do you want to stock your pantry with nutritious food your family will actually eat? In these trying times, are you focusing on your food storage?

If so, *Stock the Real Food Pantry* has you covered. Learn how a wonderfully stocked real food pantry will save you money and time—while giving you peace of mind.

Design a Dish: Save Your Food Dollars!

Would you like to learn great methods to reduce food waste? What if you could enjoy one meal for "free" each week?

Design a Dish will teach you how to make wonderful, simple dishes you can prepare day in and day out. You'll be amazed at how easy it is to nourish your family with these tasty dishes!

Resources

For additional resources and recipe details, please visit:

https://homespunoasis.com/stretchy-beans-resources/

About the Author

Millie Copper is a Wyoming wife and mama. After reading *Nourishing Traditions* in early 2009, her family began transforming their diet to whole, unprocessed, nutrient-dense foods—a little at a time, while stretching their food dollars.

Millie is passionate about sharing how, with a little creativity, anyone can transition to a real foods diet without overwhelming their food budget.

Millie began blogging at Real Food for Less Money (now HomespunOasis.com) in late 2009 and has amassed a collection of frugal recipes and methods. One of her specialties is cooking with wild game (especially antelope) and creating "Stretchy Beans." In May of 2010, she started a Weston A. Price Chapter to share traditional food, health, and farming with Central Wyoming.

Visit www.HomespunOasis.com for more information, tips, and tricks on budget-friendly real food recipes, homemaking, homesteading, preparedness, and more.